AF522650

T. Nagi Reddy Memorial Lecture

INDIAN POLITICS TODAY

AN ARGUMENT FOR SOCIALISM-ORIENTED PATH OF DEVELOPMENT

T. Nagi Reddy Memorial Lecture

INDIAN POLITICS TODAY

AN ARGUMENT FOR SOCIALISM-ORIENTED PATH OF DEVELOPMENT

Randhir Singh

Indian Politics Today
Randhir Singh

First Published, 2009

ISBN 978-81-89833-96-1 (Hb)

Published by
AAKAR BOOKS
28 E Pocket IV, Mayur Vihar Phase I, Delhi-110 091
Phone : 011-2279 5505 Telefax : 011-2279 5641
aakarbooks@gmail.com; www.aakarbooks.com

Printed at
Arpit Printographers
E-mail : arpitprinto@yahoo.com

Indian Politics Today*

One must from time to time repeat what one believes in, proclaim what one agrees with and what one condemns.

GOETHE

It is the great advangage of the new movement that we do not seck to anticipate the new world dogmatically, but rather to discover it in the ciriticism of the old... It is not our task to build up the future in advance and to settle all problems for all time; our task is ruthless criticsm of everything that exists, ruthless in the sense that the critism will not shrink either from its own conclusions or from conflict with the poers that be.

KARL MARX

The thinker's function, to contribute our share to the description of reality, to improve (so far as we may) the modes of getting things chosen and done. This is everybody's guarantee of honour in other people's thoughts. It is the sole true objectivity namely, a bias in favor of mankind.

BARROWS DUNHAM

I am grateful to the Tarimela Nagi Raddy Memorial Trust for inviting me to deliver this memorial lecture and share an argument with you. I feel honoured to be thus associated

---

* T. Nagi Reddy Memorial Lecture, delivered at Gandhi Peace Foundation, New Delhi, on November 8, 2008. This published version of the lecture includes the argument of the author's Durgabai Deshmukh Memorial Lecture for Council for Social Development, New Delhi, his inaugural address to the 'Conference on SEZs' at the Indian Institute of Advianced Study, Shimla and his keynote address to the annual session of the Indian Academy of Social Sciences at the Jamia Millia Islamia, New Delhi—all three delivered recently on similar or closely related themes.

with the memory of one of India's outstanding communist revolutionaries. I did not have the privilege of knowing Com. T. Nagi Reddy personally, but as one associated with India's communist movement since 1939, and sharing in its ups and downs including the Naxalite phase, I had admired him as a model communist revolutionary. The Nagi Reddy Memorial Trust is to be congratulated for its efforts to keep alive Nagi Reddy's legacy which is indeed a most valuable part of our people's revolutionary inheritance.

I am going to present my argument with the help of passages culled from what I have written earlier, mostly from the recently published *Crisis of Socialism: Notes in Defence of a Commitment*. (These passages also convey my views on some of the issues that figured in the day-long discussion that followed the lecture.)

Before I proceed with the lecture, force of habit as a teacher compels me make a point which even otherwise every audience deserves to have it made.

Among the excitingly significant slogans and practices of the rebel students of Paris in the late 1960s was one where they used to ask of everyone who would address them to first tell them: 'where do you speak from?' For every speaker inescapably speaks from a particular philosophical-political standpoint and owes it to his audience to publicly state it. It is only fair to acknowledge that I am going to speak from the standpoint of Marxism, rather Marxism as I understand it. For I have no pretensions to scholarship in Marxism. I picked up some on the way and have found it useful not only in my politics or profession as a teacher but in living my life as well. This last is not just a formal statement. Knowing Marx does make a difference to what sense you make of life, how you understand, live and act in the world. 'Indeed I must confess that Karl Marx made a man of me' is how George Bernard Shaw once put it. Marx, therefore, is important to me and I believe, he is important to all of us, today more so than ever before, if for no other reason than this: the world we are living in is a capitalist world, more capitalist than ever before after the Soviet collapse, and Marx more than any other human being, then or now, devoted his life to explaining the reality of this world and his achievment here remains unrivalled.

As a Marxist, I also speak as a socialist.*

Let me also add that I am going to share only a basic argument with you. For me it is important that 'the wood is not missed for the trees,' that is, the *basics* have to be clearly stated and understood to make proper sense of the details, which, however, is not to in any way underestimate the latter's importance for that is the level at which life is lived and the reality has to be ultimately grasped and engaged with; it is only to state the necessary condition for a truthful and effective engagement with this reality.

Again, I am not going to burden or bore you with statistics. The evidence for my argument is there, scattered all around us if only we are willing to see– a little reason and ability to interconnect is all that is needed.

•

---

* Necessary references apart, I am not, going to explain or discus. Marxism or socialism whose friends and enemies today are thus taken note of by the poet Hans Magnus Enzensberger, in his moving short poem, *Karl Heinrich Marx*:

I see you betrayed
by your disciples,
only your enemies
remained what they were.

Immediately, I would only suggest that 'Marxism of Karl Marx' with its scientific spirit, critical and humanist thrust needs to be distinguished from the scientistic, economistic and deterministic 'official Marxism' that once flooded in from Moscow and remains recognized as Marxism in most places. As for socialism, one is socialist because of capitalism and not Soviet Union, and socialism one seeks is not 'the actually existing socialism' that came to be built in its name in the erstwhile Soviet Union but as visualized by its classical tradition: a humane, democratically functioning society providing a superior and advanced form of freedom and self-determination to the people.

I will begin by stating that India today stands at a crossroads. With the ruling classes having openly opted for a capitalist path of development, our people confront, possibly, the hardest and most fateful choices of their long history.

To understand the crossroads we are at, that is Indian polities today, it helps to know how we have arrived where we are. It is not much remembered these days that we were very much a globalised country not so long ago. Before 1947, we were part of a global system, well-integrated into the world market economy. We were globalised but we did not like it. Our globalization then also had a name, imperialism, and we struggled against it because it meant—by virtue of its structural logic—accumulation of wealth in England and poverty in India. Like other Third World countries we wanted to get out of this globalization. This was a necessary though not sufficient condition to be able to build a better life for our people. Herein lay the essential meaning of our struggle for freedom. It is significant of our present-day rulers, including those claiming to be successors of Gandhi and Nehru, that they have long forgotten what this struggle was about and would like us all to do the same. But our people need to remember.

Aware of the exploitative logic of the global capitalist market, of centuries of experience of imperialism which provides little evidence of the beneficial effect of foreign investment in countries of the Third World so far as the common people are concerned, and in its own way influenced by the interim successes of the Soviet Union, the post-independence (Nehruvian) national project opted for the strategic goal of a state-led self reliant development, promising economic growth with 'equity and distributive justice' to the people. However, it did not work out the way it was intended. There was a significant degree of economic growth but not much equity or distributive justice for the people and the project ended up building an India-specific, government-supported capitalism. The rhetoric of 'a socialistic pattern of society' only deceived the people, legitimized the statist-capitalism that was coming up and created confusion about it as 'socialism' that persists to this day, and the failure of this capitalism to deliver was and continues to be misinterpreted as the failure of socialism in India. But the point to be immediately noted is that passing through a series of economic and political crises, the national project, such as it was, finally and definitively collapsed in 1991, foregrounding once again—now in the context of the changed balance of forces in the world following the collapse of the Soviet Union– the question of strategic options for India's future economic and social development.

This is how I assessed it all in 1997, on the occasion of the 50th anniversary of India's Independence:

> The Nehru era was the golden age of India's national project, though it was never without its critics. The slogan was 'growth with equity and distributive justice'. Acting as 'the executor of the economic necessities of the national situation', in Engels' words, the Indian state indeed ensured growth in the economy but the hope for equity and distributive justice to people was largely belied. The years that followed revealed the inherent limitations of the Nehruvian national project and saw its rapid disintegration. The structural logic of 'the existing order' prevailing, the economy was soon 'some strange kind of corrupted capitalist growth', as Romesh Thapar saw it, or 'a type of capitalist development in the interests of a narrow section of Indian society, 'as V.K.R.V. Rao put it. As it finally came up, it could be more firmly described as a state-supported India-specific capitalism which reminded one of Marx's observation about countries which
>
>> suffer not only from the development of capitalist production but also from the incompleteness of that development. Alongside of modern evils a whole series of inherited evils oppress us, arising from the passive survival of antiquated modes of production with their inevitable train of social and political anachronisms. We suffer not only from the living but from the dead.
>
> As a capitalism, its structural logic meant unequal and uneven development in the country as a whole – the near-universally

recognized 'two nations' (the rich and the poor) and 'internal colonialism' (in relation to the country's more backward parts). As for its specificity, this is how I put it sometime back:

> Its historical specificity has given it a strong comprador and lumpen character, presided over as it is by a bourgeoisie born old without ever having known youth, with none of the possible virtues of youth and all the vices of old age. Here all the exploitative and oppressive evils of belated capitalist development, semi-feudalism, bureaucratically-corrupt public sector and bloated bourgeois politics daily enter into and reinforce each other. All pervasive black money, flourishing as a parallel economy, only intensifies the structural biases of a white money of scams and swindles, even as it serves to sustain, with help from politicians, policemen and sundry state functionaries, an essentially illegal, secular or communal, mafiosi-led parallel political polity, which has today come toacquire an almost legitimized coexistence with the formally legal state in large, especially urban, parts of the country. A long time ago, apropos the essentially secondary character of such capitalist development, Karl Marx had written: 'as is well known, secondary diseases are more difficult to cure and, at the same time, ravage the body more than original ones.'

Outside of economy it was soon a case of the 'state as private property', and any kind of power in the state a means of 'rapid private accumulation'; on official admission, even of the funds directly allocated for poverty alleviation, only 'the leakage', a bare fifteen per cent, reached the people – the state in India far from being a part of any solution, itself became a part of almost every problem. Democracy, fought for and won by the people, still valuable to them, and throughout defended by them against subversion from above, yet only vindicated Bagehot's classic observation about its being 'the way to give the people the greatest illusion of power while, allowing them the smallest amount in reality', even as it also served to legtimise the ruling class domination in society. 'Democratic politics' itself, once practiced as 'Hindu Undivided Family'. as economic problems surfaced, steadily degenerated into an utterly unscrupulous, no-holds barred infighting among the beneficiaries of the system for power and pelf in the state, where, as they violated the rules of their own game, it was now truly the end justifying the means, literally any means; it was Malraux's politicians' politics' in its worst sense. The national project was fast ending up as a class project but not recognized as such. It had its beneficiaries and there was a consensus of the arrived and the complacent about it. Nationalism too had its uses, the emerging reality could be obscured in its name. Such was the domination of the ruling class ideas that even those who saw capitalism, saw it more as our very own 'national economy', and together with faith and force of habit, this ensured the prevalence of the view that the 'national project' was still on. But the project was already faltering. In any case there was nothing much in its achievements for the vast masses of the common Indian people. To borrow from Tom Paine's metaphoric rejoinder to Burke's attack on the French Revolution, the 'plumage' of India's 'national development' was yet that of a 'dying bird'. The world looked very diferent from below, when the poor and oppressed of 'our nation' looked at it. However, the definitive collapse of the national project was still in the future.

Mid-sixties onwards the post-colonial national project in India floundered and fast degenerated, its economic crises underpinning and moving in step with the crises of the political system, 'democratic politics' and all that. If India's 'national economy; generated any number of potentially explosive issues, its 'national politics' regularly turned these issues into problems, problems into running sores and these sores into tragedies for the Indian people, in Punjab, Kashmir, almost everywhere. By the end of the eighties the national project was virtually over. Soon enough, a dead-end economic crisis or financial bankruptcy of sorts, produced by the previously pursued policies, coincided with the defeat of the Soviet Union in the Cold War and its eventual disintegration, depriving the Indian ruling classes of whatever little manoeuvrability they still had, leaving them more vulnerable than ever before to the offensive of a recharged global capitalism. Given the strong comprador or lumpen strain inherent in their character, led by their major political formation, the Congress I, with their other political formations in tow, they succumbed, and hiccups and protests over 'level playing field' notwithstanding, opted for what is turning out to be a junior partnership within the global capitalist system. As beneficiaries of growth during the Nehru era and afterwards, and now with a substantial economic strength of their own, 'globalization' also provides them with new avenues of profit making at home and abroad. Therefore, this 'succumbing' can also be seen as a natural progress for Indian capitalism. India was again globalised, this time through a largely voluntary submission of the Indian rulers. The national project

> finally and definitively collapsed in 1991.
>
> The evidence of this collapse is there in the disintegration of values, and degradation life all around us, in the continuing poverty of our people and growing consumerism of the elites and a society at once cynical and fearful about the future. It is there in official statistics and pages of the private media and so-called 'national mainstream; which, bearing the impress of India's corrupt and corrupting, somewhat lumpen capitalist development, is an increasingly dirty affair – corrupt, communal and criminalized, a repressively homogenizing mainstream. The evidence is there in the visionless and so obviously laboured efforts of the powers that be to flog a tired nd flabby patriotism into some semblance of life in this fiftieth year of India's independence, including Colgate-sponsored selling of *Vande Matarams* on the television by hordes of India's VIPs and VVIPs. And this evidence is pathetically present in the impotence (or is it hypocrisy?) of the supposedly 'stirring' calls being made on the occasion – in Parliament for a 'second freedom struggle' and by the Prime Minister to 'begin the struggle for economic freedom'! One wonders what these past fifty years have been about. A Finance Minister took India back into globalization, asking us not to be afraid of the East India Company, opened up India to the multinationals, on the dishonest plea that 'the nation has been living beyond its means'– 'nation' indeed, when a good majority of our people have simply no means to live and most others none to indulge any 'living beyond'! His successor, more honest and ideologically committed. has been publicly pleading with the former globalisers in London to come back to India for another equally long stay (and then gone to town with this pleading in Washington and elsewhere): 'You came to India and stayed for 200 years. Now come prepared to invest and stay for another 200 years, and there will be huge rewards'. The post-colonial national project is indeed over and done with.

That the Nehruvian national project, contrary to its publicly professed aims or claims, ended up building a state-supported capitalism, is not difficult to understand, In large historical processes there are continuities and there are breaks, at times even revolutionary breaks which involve a change in the economic basis, the economic-structural relations, of society. In India, in our times, no revolutionary break has occurred, neither at independence, nor afterwards. The balance of social forces and ideals in the national movement resulted in the settlement of 1947 —its 'transfer of power' involving no basic economic or social or state-structural change, but putting new, now Indian ruling classes in control of the state power in India. (Nearly two decades later, Gunnar Myrdal was to write of 'the new government's role as the successor to the British raj', of 'the gulf between rulers and ruled' and the life-style and conduct of the new rulers which 'encouraged the view that political independence had done little more than displace a foregin with a native privileged group.') The new rulers set about India's economic development even as they maintained, of course, with due modifications, the class (exploitative) structure of the Indian society as a whole. It is the logic of this structure, the new and the old well articulating with each other, which had a determining influence on what eventually came to be built in the country—an India-specific state-supported capitalism, with every aspect of our social life—politics, culture, morality, everything, everywhere—bearing the mark of this somewhat comprador capitalism.

In these matters, the subjective concerns of political leaders, of rulers or their political representatives, matter—but only marginally. In the absence of revolutionary politics which changes the objective, economic-structural basis of society, not only does the logic of this basis assert itself in the economy, it also decisively conditions developments in other areas of social life, in politics, morals, culture, ideology, etc.—all changes, no matter how important otherwise, yet remain essentially superstructural. Thus, for example, we know of Gandhi's love and concern for the Indian people which to him meant, above all, the impoverished peasantry of India—'the semi-starved masses...slowly sinking to lifelessness' as he once put it—a love and concern (rather paternal in nature, always fearful of people straying from the 'right' path) which was possibly the most distinguishing feature of Gandhi's social philosophy. Metaphorically speaking, he wanted the peasant to inherit this country. Yet it is not Gandhi's peasant but a Birla who inherited India in 1947, along with, of course, communal violence, the partition, and much else that Gandhi did not want. And of decisive importance here is the fact that, besides other limitations, Gandhi's political theory and practice (non-violence, trusteeship, stayagraha, etc.) had no room at all for any genuine economic- structural change, not even for radical land reforms, a necessary though not sufficient condition for any improvement in the life of the vast masses of Indian peasantry. Inevitably he failed, here as also elsewhere in most of his declared purposes. Seeking to ensure 'the rights alike of prince and pauper', Gandhism, in effect, only served as a petty-bourgeois ideology in the service of the big bourgeoisie, in the Indian historical process. It is a mark of the greatness of Gandhi, a truly magnificent human being with all his faults, frailties and foibles, that in sharp contrast to the opportunism or pettiness of his many followers, he recognised his failure when it finally occurred, and confessed it— 'I do not understand how all these terrible things are happening in our country... What mistakes have we made, for we must have made mistakes? Otherwise how could all these things happen?'—and died, as he had lived, fighting for his people, a fulfilled yet disillusioned and disconsolate man.

Or, again, we know of Nehru's concern to build socialism in India. He not only argued that 'the only key to the solution of...India's problems lies in socialism', but had insisted: 'and when I use this word I do so not in a vague, humanitarian way, but in a scientific, economic sense'. Aware of the need for 'vast and revolutionary changes', he most perceptively spoke of 'terrible costs of not changing the existing order'. Yet, once in power, Nehru shied away from the cost of even genuine land reforms— 'they will present numerous practical problems involving basic social conflicts (and may) give rise to organised forces of disruption', the Draft Outline of the

First Five-Year Plan warned. What is more, he simply abandoned socialism 'in a scientific, economic sense', that is, as a basic economic-structural change. Apart from the insistence on the state playing 'a vital part in planning and development', the focus is increasingly on the need to ensure 'rapid economic development with continually rising levels of production', 'to exploit natural resources', 'to take sufficient advantage of the advance in science and technology', etc. In fact, in a subtle, perhaps unconscious but politically most convenient shift, he now sought 'the key' not in socialism but in the development of 'science and technology'— 'the temples of modern India' and all that. He increasingly opted for what I would describe as 'fetishism of science', that is, investing science with powers it does not in-itself have, expecting it to do the job of a social revolution, which it simply cannot. Inevitably, once again, the logic of the economic structure asserted itself. What got built in India was not socialism but capitalism, a state-supported capitalism. The rhetoric of socialism, now redefined as 'a socialistic pattern of society', whatever that meant, served only to deceive and win mass support. And Nehru, even as he gave India the then much-lauded 'vision of socialism', in effect, helped reduce it to only 'a vision' in India. History is indeed a very cruel mistress.

•

The post-independence national project having collapsed, 1991 onwards, India's ruling classes, through their different political formations, notably the Congress and the BJP, have gone in for 'globalisation' as their new strategic option – a shift from the state-supported capitalism to a privatised 'free market' capitalism and from self-reliance in economic development to reliance on Foreign Direct Investment and the multinationals, a shift euphemistically described as 'economic reforms' which has little to offer to the common Indian people. The much-touted 'growth rates' are no indication of general well-being in a capitalist society; instead, as Amit Bhaduri has pointed out, 'the unprecedented high economic growth on which privileged India prides itself is a measure of the high speed at which India of privilege is distancing itself from the India of crushing proverty... the higher the rate of economic growth along this pattern becomes, the greater would be underdevelopment of India'. The so-called 'trickle down', if and when it occurs, is no better than 'feeding the horses with oats so that some of it passes down to the road for the sparrows', as Galbraith once described it. Over the past decade-and-a-half or so, whatever be the benefits 'economic reforms' has brought to a small section at the top, it has further polarised our society, played havoc with the lives of our common people and pushed them still further into a peripheralised existence within the global capitalist system, with the Special Economic Zones (SEZs) making their own specific contribution to this ruination of the common man. Describing if all as 'developmental terrrorism', Amit Bhaduri has written: 'Destruction of livelihoods and displacement of the poor in the name of industrialisation, big dams for power generation and irrigation, corporatisation of agriculture despite farmers' suicides, modernization and beautification of our cities by demolishing slums are showing everyday how development can turn perverse... The devil in angel's guise would soon appear when large populations in rural India would be rendered landless, jobless, homeless, incomeless, rootless and displaced making way for gargantuan SEZs. the so-called epitomes of economic developoment.'

This is nothing surprising 'Economic reforms' is only a euphemism for capitalist development whose structural logic, as a former President of Brazil once reported it to the masters in Washington, is: 'the economy is doing fine, the people are not'. Chary of using the word 'capitalism', even the advocates of globalisation, Joseph Stiglitz, Amartya Sen and others, regularly admit and lament that 'the fruits of globalisation' are not reaching the people, and Klaus Schwab (of the World Economic Forum) writes: 'We are living in an increasingly schizophrenic world, where economies are booming and global signs are promising, but underneath are political and social risks, as well as imbalances and inconsistencies.' SEZs, as a part of country's capitalist development, is development at the cost of the people, above all the small peasant – a process akin to what Marx, in his account of the genesis and development of capitalism in the West, noticed as 'primitive accumulation of capital' which apart from the colonial plunder, slavery and massacres of indigenous populations, included mass uprooting of peasantry by force and legislation. Marx has written:

> The capitalist system presupposes the complete separation of the labourers from all property in the means by which they can realise their labour... a process that transforms, on the one hand, the social means of subsistence and of production into capital, onthe other, the immediate producers into wage labourers. This historical process... appears as primitive, because it forms the pre-historic stage of capital...
>
> (Most basic in this process are)
>
> those moments when great masses of men are suddenly and forcibly torn from their means of subsistence, and hurled as free and 'unattached' proletarians on the labour market... law itself becomes... the instrument of the theft of the people's land... The history of this expropriation, in different countries, assumes different aspects, and runs through its various phases in different orders of succession, and at different periods...

A market-governed economic growth simply cannot deliver 'inclusive growth', to use another of the proliferating buzzwords of our time. Instead, it is by its very nature exclusionary and the logic of the market, with its inevitable winners and losers, only makes for 'the secession of the successful', as the economist Robert Reich once phrased it. One look at their economic policies or concerns. their lifestyles and values will reveal how far 'the successful' of India's marketplace have already 'seceded' from the vast majority of their supposedly 'unsuccessful' fellow countrymen. Incidentally, market-governed, that is, capitalist industrialisation is claimed to be an answer to the problem of unemployment in the country. This, when unemployment, inherent in the very workings of capitalism, its capital accumulation process, has now come to stay as a permanent feature of the economy in the advanced capitalist countries, recognised and argued for by bourgeois ideologues as 'structural unemployment', a necessary condition for the economy to be in equilibrium and functional, with Milton Friedman even coining a scientific sounding term for this new orthodoxy, 'a natural rate of unemployment,' a rate that is built into the very structure of the economy! This apart, it should he obvious that corporate-led industrialisation generally does not generate much employment. Even as it simultaneously destroys employment in activities supplanted by it and its offshoots, its primary concern with profit-making involves cutting costs including labour costs. It is indeed an illusion that corporate industrialisation with its labour-saving automated technologies can ever generate *net* employment opportunities. As to the promise of 'indirect' employment created in the wake of industry, it has been well described as 'a pie in the sky for the peasants'. Above and beyond all this is the overarching issue of *the quantity and even more the quality* of employment in this age of globalisation, with its 'jobless growth', ruthless competition in the markets at home and abroad, and vast masses of our people reduced to be 'the reserve army of labour'for national and global capitalism.

Apropos India's state-supported capitalist development during the Nehru era and later. I had written:

> To borrow from Tom Paine's metaphoric rejoinder to Burke's attack on the French revolution, admiration for the 'plumage' of India's 'national development' should not prevent us from seeing its failure in 'the dying bird'. The world indeed looks very different from below, when the poor and oppressed of 'our nation' look at it.

This is even more true of the market-led capitalist development during the current era of neo-liberal 'economic reforms'.

•

Before proceeding with my argument about what I have elsewhere described as 'contemporary India's most important *unraised* political question', the question of a people's strategic option, an alternative path of development distinct from and in opposition to that of India's ruling classes, I would like to touch upon a few aspects or implications of the current shift to globalisation or 'economic reforms' which are immediately relevant to several important issues of the present-day Indian politics.

Obviously, the most important aspect here concerns the concept of 'globalisation', whose centrality in contemporary economic and political discourse calls for a somewhat detailed comment.

A buzzword for 40 odd years now 'globalisation' is far from being an unambiguous or conceptually clear theoretical construct. Given the fuzziness of language over it. Peter Marcuse has even called it a 'non-concept': 'a simple catalogue of everything that seems different since say 1970, whether advances in information technology widespread use of air freight, speculation in currencies, increased capital flows across borders, Disneyfication of culture, mass marketing, global warming, genetic engineering multinational corporate power, new international division of labour, international mobility of labour, reduced power of nation-states, postmodernism, or post-Fordism.' But this is not all. As Peter Marcuse adds: 'The issue is more than one of careless use of words: intellectually, such muddy use of the term fogs any effort to separate cause from effect, to analyze what is being done, by whom, to whom, for what, and with what effect. Politically, leaving the term vague and ghostly permits its conversion to something with a life of its own, making it a force, fetishizing it as something that has an existence independent of the will of human beings, inevitable and irresistible.'

Thus, for its ardent ideologue Thomas Friedman— a big time columnist of the *New York Times*—globalisation is a new technological-economic system based in the microchip and ruled by an 'electronic herd' of financial investors and multinational corporations, sweeping away everything that came before—capitalism and socialism, the nation-state, imperialism, class struggle, everything. And we have even well-meaning mainstream scholars coming up with what can at best be described as deceptively confusing interpretations. For John Harriss, for example, 'globalisation' is a recent phenomena. He views the use of the term 'in the last 10 years or so' as 'an indication that something has been happening out there', and goes on to describe it in conventional fuzzy terms: '...the world is more inter-connected and supposedly more interdependent than it was formerly, as a result of changes in the global economy–notably rapid movements of large volumes of money and the increased volume of trade–as well as of changes in communications and in information technology. These trends are related in turn and more controversially, with a variety of political and cultural changes, including perhaps especially the ideas of "deterritorialisation", of the decline of the nation state and of a shift to politics of presence.' For Amartya Sen globalisation is almost as old as civilisation itself: 'Over thousands of years, globalisation has progressed through travel, trade, migration, spread of cultural influences and dissemination of knowledge (including of science and technology)'. Sen recognises 'the dual presence of abject misery and unprecedented prosperity in the world in which we live'— 'incomparably richer than ever before, ours is also a world of extraordinary deprivation and staggering inequality'— to end up urging support for globalisation 'in the best sense of that idea', and pleading: 'what is needed is a fairer distribution of the fruits of globalisation'. Globalisation's historically specific reality today is evaded through an appeal to its so-called 'idea in the best sense', which only adds to the prevailing fuzziness and confusion in the use of this term or concept.

Be that as it may, there are many reasons to doubt that 'globalisation' represents an accurate account of the phenomena it purports to describe. On the other hand, there are good reasons to treat it, in its current usage, as ideological mystification of the reality of our times.

As a theoretical concept, globalisation came up in the late 1960s and early 1970s to account for a recent complex of developments in the global economy, particularly the major expansion and conquest of markets by the multinationals, seeking to present this international capitalist expansion in a favourable light, an alternative to Marxist vocabulary with its concepts of imperialism, capitalism, etc. In its current widely accepted usage, acquiring new credibility with the collapse of 'Soviet socialism', the concept is characterised by two distinct emphases. In the first place, linked to what has been called the third technological revolution, this internationalisation of capital has come to be viewed as a tide sweeping over borders in which technology and irresistible market forces transform the global system in ways beyond the power of anyone to do much to change. The view is often buttressed by a kind of technological determinism where the new electronic technologies make globalisation not only possible or necessary, but inevitable. Globalisation is viewed as an entity in itself, an inevitable, irreversible natural process, which independently of any human will or politics is now taking over and transforming the world. In its second distinctive emphasis, globalisation is seen as a historical rupture of a qualitative kind from the changes that have been occurring in capitalism since its inception. The changes now taking place represent a distinctive and unique kind of 'epochal shift' a notion which these days runs as a kind of *leitmotif* through a wide spectrum of intellectual currents, where 'post' is the presiding buzzword. We are told that we are now, since the early 1970s to be precise, living through an epochal shift, the birth of a new era, a major qualitative leap so different from the earlier changes in the process of capitalist development that the very logic of capitalism stands superseded. In the globalised world of today there is no capitalism with its exploitation and oppressions, its classes and class struggles, its structural defects and explosive antagonisms, its chronic problems or crises. Imperialism too is now a thing of the past. As such, globalization is also argued for as a benevolent phenomenon, an almost automatic solution to all the encountered problems and contradictions of our economy, if not our society as a whole—very much like the once similarly hailed and revered notion of 'invisible hand', Adam Smith's assurance that went so grievously sour as soon as the logic of *capitalist* market asserted itself.

Around this notion of a technology-driven 'globalisation' has grown a new orthodoxy, that of 'a dematerialised world', which yet again suggests supersession of capitalism as an economic system and therefore obsolescence of the associated categories of analysis. In a recent article, speaking of 'the Myth of Weightless Economy', Ursula Huws has written:

> 'The Death of Distance' 'Weightless World' the 'Connected Economy', the 'Digital Economy', the 'Knowledge-Based Economy', the 'Virtual Organization'. All these phrases were culled from the titles of books published in the six months prior to writing this essay, in spring, 1998. They could have been multiplied many times: 'virtual', 'cyber', 'tele-', 'networked' or even just 'e' can, it seems, be prefixed interchangeably to an almost infinite range of abstract nouns. Without even straying from the field of economics, you can try 'enterprise', 'work', 'banking', 'trade' 'commerce' or 'business' (although the device works equally well in other areas: for instance 'culture', 'politics', 'sex', 'democracy', 'relationship', 'drama', 'community', 'art', 'society', 'shopping' or 'crime').
>
> A consensus seems to be emerging – in economics as in other

> fields – that something entirely new is happening: that the world as we know it is becoming quite dematerialised (or, as Marx put it, 'all that is solid melts into air') and that this somehow throws into question all the conceptual models which have been developed to make sense of the old material world. We are offered a paradoxical universe: geography without distance, history without time, value without weight, transactions without cash. This is an economics which sits comfortably in a Baudrillardian philosophical framework, in which all reality has become a simulacrum and human agency, to the extent that it can be said to exist at all, is reduced to the manipulation of abstractions...

The ideological-political implications are obvious. As in the current conventional conception of 'globalisation', capitalism, the historically specific capitalist processes, the capitalist exploitation of human beings and natural resources, simply disappear. The frenetic and feverish manner in which the information revolution is hyped, makes it appear that the entire system of organised capitalism dating back to Industrial Revolution (and even earlier) is being displaced by a new age of 'the electronic republic' and 'digital futurologies' where information or 'knowledge' is the only source of value and work is something contingent and delocalisable if not dispensable, where the demand or need to produce material means of living, indeed any assertion of the physical claims of the human body in the here-and-now is an old-fashioned concern, where 'the computer', lord and master of it all, refashions economy and society, human beings themselves, in its own image.

As capitalism goes out of sight, 'globalisation' as a universal category of analysis displaces the critical socialist concepts of 'capitalism', or 'imperialism', and together with its technological determinism undercuts any notion of radical or systemic transformative politics. Any kind of anti-capitalist project is ruled out. A natural, inevitable process, any resistance to 'globalisation' is futile. There is no alternative but accept its dictates. 'Globalisation' thus disarms any opposition to almighty capital, becomes an ideological tool instilling a certain fatalism in the working people, nations and states to induce them to follow policies of adjustment to the demands of global capitalism, at home and abroad.

The conventional theorising over 'globalisation'—'globloney' it has been called– mystifies the reality of our world. Postulating an utterly fictitious world of superseded capitalism, it makes capitalism safe against criticism and opposition and using the argument of 'inevitability', it wants us to believe that in this globalised world there is no alternative to the meek acceptance of the conditions necessary for its trouble-free functioning, which in effect means trouble-free functioning of the global capitalist system.

It only needs to be added that today quite a few on the left, indeed a painfully large majority, too has succumbed to the infashion 'globloney' of the right. This left has presently joined the right in accepting that 'There Is No Alternative' – not just no alternative to capitalism but to a more or less (the right goes for more, the left somewhat less) ruthlessly 'flexible' capitalism.

Globalisation, however, is nothing qualitatively new in the history of bourgeois society, it is a process that has been going on for a long time, in fact ever since capitalism came into the world as a viable form of society four or five centuries ago. An ever-changing system, capitalism was born and grew, and grew to maturity only as a world system. In other words, capitalism has always been a global or globalising system, one moving inexorably towards 'globlisation' from its very inception. The most significant elements of what is called globalisation have always been part of capitalist development, even if the specific forms and features of this development including globalisation – that is, the global process of capital expansion and accumulation – have been different in different periods (including our own). That capitalism is in its innermost essence an expanding system both internally and externally was pointed out by Marx a long time ago. Once rooted, propelled by the law of accumulation of capital, it both grows and spreads. The classic analysis of this double movement is of course Marx's *Capital*. But the *globalising* nature of capitalism was diagnosed and emphasised by him more than 150 years ago in the *Communist Manifesto* itself. Marx has been proved uncannily right about many things but perhaps nowhere has he been vindicated more completely than in his accournt of capitalist expansion or globalisation. Here, for example, are a couple of passages from the *Manifesto*: 'The bourgeosie has through its exploitation of the world market given a cosmopolitan character to production and consumption in every country... All old-established national industries have been destroyed or are being destroyed. They are dislodged by new industries, whose introduction becomes a life and death question for all nations, by industries that no longer work up indigenous raw material, but raw material drawn from the remotest zones: industries whose products are consumed not only at home, but in every quarter of the globe. In place of the old wants, satisfied by the productions of the country, we find new wants, requiring for their satisfaction the products of distant lands and climes... in place of the old local and national seclusion and self-sufficiency, we have intercourse in every direction, universal interdependence of nations...' Again: 'The need of a constantly expanding market for its productions chases the bourgeoisie over the whole surface of the globe. It must nestle everywhere, settle everywhere, establish connections everywhere...' Yet again: the bourgeoisie 'batters down all Chinese walls' and 'compels all nations, on pain of extinction, to adopt the bourgeois mode of production; it compels them to introduce what it calls civilisation into their midst, i.e... to become bourgeois themselves. In one word, it creates a world after its own image'. Of course, these passages from the *Communist Manifesto* (1848) are not a simple description of contemporary reality. A statement of general and long-term processes that have been part of capitalist development from the beginning, they are more an anticipation of the future that is ours today. They represent an analysis which is much truer today than when the *Manifesto* was composed. It is true that Marx underestimated the durability of capitalism and how long it could keep on expanding. But for all today's fashionable talk about 'globalisation', it would be hard to find a more effective description of what is happening today than what he wrote 150 odd years ago.

Marx's is analytically the most sophisticated recognition of capitalism as a system that is uniquely expansionary and international, one tangentially 'global' since the very beginning, but a more than working recognition of this dimension of capitalism was common to classical thinkers such as Adam Smith, and later to most mainstream economists before the first world war. Multinational manufacturing firms appeared in the middle of the 19th century and were well established by the beginning of the 20th century to make internationalisation of capital a common preoccupation not only of Marxist theorists like Luxemburg. Lenin or Bukharin. Analysts have pointed out that foreign trade and overseas income was a greater percentage of GNP in Europe during the late 19th century than at the end of the 20th century, that world financial markets in the late 19th and early 20th centuries were more fully integrated than they were before or have been since. As a commentator for the *Financial Times* of London has recently put it: 'Before 1914 the world economy was in many respects as integrated as it is today and in certain respects more so'. This integration, with capital and commodities freely traversing the globe, had also made for internationalisation of social and economic life. This is how John Maynard Keynes saw it: 'The inhabitant of London could order by telephone, sipping his morning tea in bed, the various products of the whole earth, in such quantity as he might see fit, and resonably expect their early delivery upon his doorstep; he could at the same moment and by the same means adventure his wealth in the natural resources and new enterprises in any quarter of the world, and share, without exertion or even trouble, in their prospective fruits and advantages; or he could decide to couple the security of his fortunes with the good faith of the townspeople of any substantial municipality in any continent that fancy or information might recommend. He could secure forthwith, if he wished it, cheap and comfortable means of transit to any country or climate without passport or other formality... But, most important of all, he regarded this state of affairs as normal, certain, and permanent, except in the direction of improvement... The internationalization of (social and economic life) was nearly complete...' Thus, if 'globalization' is no novelty in the history of capitalist development, the associated notion of 'a borderless world' too is no recent invention.

There is an unending hype, 'infobabble' really, over information technology which, together with globalisation it has so remarkably facilitated, is supposed to usher in the epochal shift that takes us into a world beyond and better than capitalism, indeed makes the very notion of capitalism historically irrelevant. Involving two closely linked technological departure points, the computer and instantaneous communication system, a fusion as it were of computing and communications (*networks*) that has developed in an explosive trajectory in recent years, this technological development has been not unjustifiably described as a revolution, 'information revolution', that is. The importance, however ambiguous, of this revolution for our economy and social life is not to be denied. For good or ill, it has enormously significant implications for the present and future of humankind – implications that socialists need to take serious note of. As Reg Whitaker, in a most perceptive essay on the subject, has insisted 'this revolustion cannot be ignored by those seeking real alternatives. Cyberspace is a new reality, a spectre haunting the world. As some of the old terrains of struggle shrink, cyberspace expands as a new terrain to be studied, and to be acted upon.' But this revolution itself does not either change the structural logic of capitalism or offer, or make for, any alternatives to the present social order.

New information technology, as with technological innovations in the past, certainly makes people better at doing things they have always done. But even here we don't need to be breathless about it. It is difficult to see how, as claimed, the nature of manufacturing has been 'fundamentally altered' by it. The evidence so far shows only very small impact on productivity from the large investment made in information technology in the United States or for that matter elsewhere. Production has indeed been globalised, but it remains doubtful if the telecommunications revolution has really had a major impact. It has been suggested that 'the invention of relatively simple things, like steamship transport, did more for world trade than digitalised data transmission through fiber optic cables.' In other words, its truly remarkable technological innovations and the hype over them notwithstanding, in the ultimate analysis. 'information revolution' is only another case of incremental change in the way we do things.

'Information revolution' is emphatically not itself an answer to the problems we face – problems primarily born of capitalism and its structural logic. These are problems we ourselves have to solve, with or without the aid of technology. 'Information is power', or the computer as 'empowerment', do have a certain, though ambigous, validity. But 'infobabble' over such propositions has little to do with any notion of redistribution of wealth and power in our society. A computer in every office or home will not some how solve the problem of unemployment or economic crisis or regional economic decline and imbalances. The poor cannot 'unload' from the

NET food and shelter or equitable economic development they are denied by the capitalist market. Information technology does not and cannot in any way alter capital's drive to accumulate or its quest for higher profits and stock prices. Instead it has only served to make this quest more penetrating and effective. As with other technologies under capitalism, information technology too is today subservient to capitalist imperatives of accumulation and profit maximisation. Command over information and its transmission has already become the key to success in the capitalist marketplace. A wholesale commodification of information by capital is on and the much celebrated 'cyberspace' is taking on the appearance of a 'vast mysterious collections of data looming like mega-fortresses fiercely guarded by giant corporations – while the "real world" wallows in urban squalor, petty criminality, violence and tawdry escapism.' This is how Reg Whitaker has posed and answered the key question: 'Does the Information Revolution ofter an alternative? Yes and no. It does offer an alternative capitalist future, but it is unlikely, under present circumstance, to offer an alternative to capitalism.'

Capitalist development, given the contradictions inherent in capitalism, has always been a crisis- ridden, bumpy and uneven affair. It is no different with globalisation as a capitalist process. Its progress to has been essentially bumpy and uneven, and shot through with local, regional and more than regional crises. There have been periods of 'high' globalisation and periods in which economic flows have, to a greater or lesser degree, turned inward in response to changed economic and political conditions. Thus, the second half of the nineteenth century witnessed an escalating thrust of 'globalisation' as a part of capitalism's normal existence. It continued in the twentieth century and globalisation was really intense until 1914. Two world wars, a great depression, revolution in Russia and working class struggles somewhat interrupted this trend, creating what Hobsbawn has described as an interlude of national economics between eras of international economics. This interlude saw the domestic economies, turn in on themselvs and there was a prolonged shift to a period of 'national development,' of 'largely delinked, managed national economies', as one description has it – the so-called Keynesian era which was the unique product of a catastrophic period for capitalism in the first half of the twentieth century. Once a certain degree of economic and political recovery was achieved, there was an inceasing and uneven effort from the 1950s onwards to return to active globalisation. The effort picked up with the onset of the crisis in the 1970s, when together with a return to its normal functioning at home, capitalism resumed its path towards internationalisation with a vengeance, to be soon provided a new specific thrust by the collapse in the East. The erosion and disintegration of Keynesianism (with its regulated capitalism and welfare state) and the onset of so-called 'globalisation' not only reflected the depth of the new crisis but also demonstrated capital's inherent, and now increasingly desperate, drive to create a world economy 'in its own image'. Such has been the changing trajectory of globalisation in our time.

Viewed in this perspective, the increasing integration of national economies and the globalisation of trade and investment are not new phenomena, only a new phase in the normal existence of capitalism as a global system. What has taken place, far from being some new departure, is rather a return, a turning back to trends that marked the 'high' globalisation of the nineteenth century, a resumption of the drive that had temporarily slowed down during the intervening period of 'low' globalisation. And with this resumed globalisation, given the depth of the current economic crisis, we are also back– with a new vengeance this time – to pre-Keynesian economics and ideological hegemony of *laissez faire*.

•

The talk about 'globalisation' as 'a new era' or 'an epochal shift' represents more an ideological-political phenomenon than a serious analysis of the new situation. What is important, therefore, is not to indulge in such talk but to notice the specificities of the current phase of globalization, each of which can be seen to be directly relevant to what is happening in Indian politics today—all that is needed, as I said earleier, is a little reason and ability to interconnect.

In the sphere of economy proper, the most important specificity to be noticed about the current phase of globalization is its radical departure from the way capitalism existed during the previous period of post-war boom., the 'golden age' of capitalism. Capitalism of this period was marked by Keynesian strategies of moderate macro-economic regulations and the accompanying limits on capital's unending thirst for more profits, collectively known as the 'welfare state' which, incidentally, saved capitalism from its own self-destructive tendencies – as manifested, for example, in the Great Depression– and also helped it acquire a much-needed 'human face' against the internal and external threat of socialism. The onset of a structural crisis of capitalism, which gives every sign of being irreversible, has changed all that. 1970s saw the world economy going into a downturn that has worsened through every recession since; the gap between business cycles is getting smaller, barely does recovery begin, the growth falters. 'Globalisation', with its neo-liberalism, is essentially a response to this structural crisis of capitalism and signifies a return, as it were, from an atypical to typical capitalism, from the aberration that was the post-war 'golden age'; with its welfare state to a period of normal, 'free-market' capitalism. For capital to remain 'competitive' in the global market, Keynesian state interventions in the economy have to go. Nor can capitalism now afford to wear a 'human face'; with the threat of socialism having receded, perhaps, it also does not need to wear it any more. The exceptional circumstances that made it possible for the working classes in the West, especially Western Europe, to fight and curb the exploitative logic of capitalism have passed into history. That these working classes are today fighting to defend their hard won gains should not obscure the fact that even in the advanced capitalist West it is no longer capitalism with a human face but back to the laws of the jungle of a normal capitalism. The state must revert to its traditional way of serving capitalism, that is, it must now act as the main agent of globalisation. And this is indeed how the state is now acting.

'Globalisation' abroad has its own specificity in the new phase. If at home 'globalisation' is capitalism alll over again, albeit now showing itself in its nakedness, abroad it is imperialism all over again, albeit in a new shape or form, when the logic of capitalism now become more or less universal, imperialism achieves its ends not so much by the old forms of physical occupation or military expansion but primarily by unleashing and manipulating the exploitative and destructive impulses of the capitalist market. This however is not to deny the continuing importance of wars or the use of military means for imperialist purposes. We have the most obvious contemporary example of the United States' use of its military power to grab control of the oil resources of the Middle-East and Central Asia and to establish pax-Americana in the world, that is, keep the world 'free' as a freely exploitable area in which giant American corporations can do business on their own terms.

Beyond these two specific features, globalization in its current phase has an aspect to it which needs to be specifically noted. Post-Soviet collapse, capitalism's impulse to globalise or universalise has so realized itself that capitalism is today a truly global or universal system, such as it has never been before. This has meant universalisation of its polarizations between the rich and the poor, the exploiters and the exploited. Its success, so to speak, has carried its failures with it, which however is nothing new or surprising. This is how it has always been with capitalism – exceptional productivity and most inequitable distribution, production of wealth and poverty at the two poles of society. More significant, however, is another consequence of universalisation: a sharpening of capitalism's contradictions and self-destructive tendencies, including the inherent tendency to overproduce, to regular crises of overproduction. Historically,. capitalism could and was indeed able to resolve or 'displace' these contradictions and escape the consequences of its self-destructive tendencies primarily by deeper penetration within and expansion abroad. To the extent it has become universal, the old escape routes are now that much less available. As Ellen Meiksins Wood has written:

> Now, capitalism has no more escape routes, no more safety valves or corrective mechanisms outside its own internal logic. Even when it's not at war, even when it's not involved in the old forms of inter-imperialist rivalry, it's subject to the constant tensions and contradictions of capitalist competition. Now, having more or less reached its geographic limits and ended the spatial expansion that supported its earlier successes, it can only feed on itself; and the more successful it is on its own terms – in other words, the more it maximizes profit and so-called growth – the more it devours its own human and natural substance.

The ultimate success of capitalism, its universal ascendancy, has also brought it to the brink of its worst failure. This condition is an important component of the structural crisis – a 'depressed continuum' Meszaros has called it – that today grips global capitalism. That some countries are doing well even in the midst of this crisis, or have cyclical upswings, is something that has happened throughout the history of capitalism and does not negate the reality of this crisis, the intractable problems that capitalism as a global system is now faced with.

Of course, capitalism today is not as Marx saw and studied it in the nineteenth century. It has undergone changes, important changes, since then, and it is necessary to recognize them for understanding and struggling against, contemporary capitalism. But as Raymond Williams once warned, in taking note of what has changed in capitalism, we must not make the mistake of underestimating everything that has not changed. And this 'everything', above all, includes the structural logic of capitalism, the law-like tendencies of its capital-accumulation process which, as Marx explicated, have meant uneven and unequal development within and across countries. The universalisation of capital does not mean the universalisation of capitalist prosperity, success, industrialisation or development, as promised by the globalisers. On the contrary, it can only mean the universalisation of capitalist polarisation, for such is the structual logic of capitalist development. And this is precisely what has been happening. Capitalism's tendency to generate wealth for the relatively few and poverty for the many is as much in evidence today in both the 'developed' North and the 'developing' South as it was in the 19th century England of 'dark satanic mills' that Marx and Engels so perceptively analysed. Now, as then, the poor grow poorer as the rich grow richer. Polarisation abroad has meant the marginalisation and increasing impoverishment of whole regions outside the advanced capitalist countries. The class polarisations of capitalism are as much evident in the North-South divide as in the growing impoverishment of the so-called 'underclasses' within advanced capitalist countries.

Finally we may here specifically notice a key feature of contemporary globalisation that it retains from its earlier phases: its driving forces are centred in the imperial states and the dominant classes within these states who own or control and run the multinational corporations and banks duly backed by the international financial institutions. Thus we have, as in the past. 'globalising' nations and classes and the 'globalised', a hierarchical system of power, exchange and benefits: there are wealthy creditors and bankrupt debtors, super rich speculators and impoverished peasants and unemployed workers, imperial states that direct international financial institutions and subordinate states that submit to their dictates, and so on. There has been much 'globaloney' over 'interdependence of nations' and its 'globally shared benefits'. Surely 'imperialism' is a more useful concept to comprehend this aspect of the reality of our globalised world.

Skewed distribution of benefits is however only one issue. 'Globalisation' is really the globalisation of capitalism's basic dynamics, including the contradictions inherent in its relentless drive to maximise profits and accumulate. As a consequence we not only have a ravaging of humanity, mass unemployment and underemployment and active impoverishment of large populations at the centre and in the periphery of global capitalism and a destruction of natural environment all over the globe but also a global economy characterised by over accumulation, enormous excess capacity and crisis of profitability, an ever-growing structure of debt, speculative volatility and financial turmoils and typically, by recurring economic crises and prolonged downturns like the current one. By virtue of its inherent contradictions, though globally dominant, capitalism yet remain fraught with instabilities., beset as it is by economic breakdowns even in its most dynamic centres of investment and trade and by a succession of national and regional crises – in Mexico. East and South-East Asia. Russia, Brazil, Argentina, etc.– produced by the globalist restructuring of recent decades.

In the sphere of politics, 'Globalisation is only another word for U.S. domination' as Henry Kissinger has arrogantly claimed. From the other end, posing the issue equally bluntly. Fredric Jameson has written: '...when we talk about the spreading power and influence of globalization aren't we really referring to the spreading economic and military might of the US? And in speaking of the weakening of the nation-state, are we not actually describing the subordination of the other nation-states to American power, either through consent and collaboration, or by the use of brute force and economic threat?' He adds: 'Looming behind the anxieties expressed here is a new version of what used to be called imperialism, which we can now trace through a whole dynasty of forms. An earlier version was that of the pre-First World War colonialist order, practised by a number of European countries, the US and Japan; this was replaced after the Second World War and the subsequent wave of decolonization by a Cold War form, less obvious but no less insidious in its use of economic pressure and blackmail ('advisers'; covert putsches such as those in Guatemala and Iran), now led predominantly by the US but still involving a few Western European powers. Now perhaps we have a third stage, in which the United States pursues what Samuel Huntington has defined as a three-pronged strategy: nuclear weapons for the US alone; human rights and American-style electoral democracy; and (less obviously) limits to immigration and the free flow of labour. One might add a fourth crucial policy here: the propagation of the free market across the globe...' Jameson sees 'the US (and such utterly subordinated satellites as the UK)' as playing 'the role of the world's policemen' and enforcing 'their rule through selected interventions (mostly bombings, from a great height) in various alleged danger zones.'

In its pursuit of global domination America has, more evidently than ever before, emerged and self-identified itself, as the country with the power and responsibility to police the world in defence of capitalism. A leading diplomatic historian, Gerald Haines (who is also the senior historian of the CIA) has observed that after World War II, the United State assumed, out of self-interest, responsibility for the welfare of the world capitalist system'. President Clinton and his Secretary of State Madeleine Albright saw US as the world's only 'indispensable nation' and Anthony Lake, his National Security Advisor, in line with a former such Advisor Brezhenski's public defence of the 'necessity' of American leadership in the world, even announced a so-called 'Clinton

Doctrine': 'Throughout the Cold War, we contained a global threat to market democracies', now we can 'consolidate the victory of democracy and open markets' the formula however is redundant since the latter adequately captures what is really meant by 'democracy'. More recently (1999), in his much noticed 'Manifesto for the Fast World' in the *New York Times Magazine*, the well-known columnist Thomas Friedman has argued that since the United States is the country that benefits most from globlization, it is also the one that has to take the main responsibility for sustaining it. 'Sustaining globalization is our overarching national interest... Globalization-is-U.S.' This, he clarifies, is different from 'old-fashioned imperialism, when one country physically occupies another'. Now, it's a matter of maintaining 'an abstract globalization system.' And this 'requires a stable geopolitical power structure, which simply cannot be maintained without the active involvement of the United States.' Bush Junior has since, in his own way, made abundantly clear what this means.

The US domination today has an interesting ideological dimension in that America has sought a 'noble' or 'saintly' guise for its policies abroad. It pursues them in the name of 'human rights' and 'democracy' which only reveals how cynical or hypocritical the sole superpower's global politics can be. Take the UN Declaration of Human Rights, Half of it concerns social and economic rights. The West largely rejects them, the US totally. They limit themselves primarily to what they call civil and political rights. This apart, if the record of the UN on human rights is painfully bad, it is understandably so because it has been, and still is, dominated by the United States, the country with innumerable violations of human rights all over the world, from the Philippines at the turn of the last century to installing Marcos there after the war, from the invasion of Guatemala, the Dominican Republic and Grenada to the Vietnam war, from installing Suharto in Indonesia (and more than one million murdered in the course of Suharto's US-backed counter-revolution) to imposing and sustaining dictatorial regimes in Latin America (including Pinochet in Chile) and Africa, not to mention the authoritarian regimes in the Middle-East, the Colonel's Dictatorship in Greece and the death of one million children in Iraq as a result of sanctions continued to be imposed by the United States and rubber-stamped by the U.N., with the total subservience of its allies, before it again attacked Iraq in a blatant violation of international law. America's interpretation of human rights, replacing the common interests of humanity with the particular intersts and arbitrary actions of the United States, violates any meaningful conception of human rights. Even otherwise America's extremely selective concern with human rights in pursuit of its interests abroad has been justifiably regarded as a new form of imperialism. 'Human Right Imperialism.'

It is no different with America's concern for democracy. The essential criterion once again is what best serves American interests. American policy makers have had no hesitation in lining up on their side some of the most corrupt dictatorial regimes that there were, often hailing them as members of their 'free world'. These have included the apartheid regime of South Africa. Syngman Rhee and the military rulers of South Korea. Ferdinand Marcos of the Philippines. Lon Nol and other dictators of South Vietnam. Ayub Khan and Yahya Khan of Pakistan, the Shah of Iraq, the Duvaliers of Haiti. Pinochet of Chile. Suharto of Indonesia and any number of other tyrants or authoritarian rulers in Africa. Central and South America and the Middle East, including once upon a time. Saddam Hussein in Iraq. It is to them that American aid and armaments have overwhelmingly gone. 'He may be a son of a bitch, but he is our-son-of-a -bitch'. This has been Washington's refreshingly honest view of the Somozas. Batistas and Duvaliers of the world. Obviously, the absence of democracy is alright so long as a country is supportive of the United States. 'Democracy' like 'human rights' is only an ideological cover for the pursuit of America's more mundane material, that is, imperialist interests abroad.

Ideological deception has its uses, no doubt, but there is nothing like exercise of naked military power to secure and sustain particular imperialist interests and overall global hegemony. With the collapse of the Soviet Union, the United States has acquired a global dominance as the one remaining military super power, indeed the dominant imperialist power in the world. Contrary to the notion that globalisation and the establishment of the world market have made military power redundant, the US maintains, by a very wide margin, the world's largest military. Empires throughout human history have relied on foreign military bases to enforce their rule and protect their interests, and in this respect Pax Americana is no different from Pax Romana or Pax Britannica. The United States has military bases in more than sixty-nine countries, with this number on the increase with the wars against Afghanistan and Iraq. The United States totally dominates NATO – recently redefined as a self-legitimating aggressive force – as well as the far eastern military alliances, especially the 'US-Japan security treaty'. Despite the publicly proclaimed end of the Cold War, the US military budget remain very large, accounting for fully a third of world spending on arms. For the US ruling class, in view of what it sees as its responsibilities in the global capitalist order – which one scholar has summarised as: 'to keep the system functioning; to control the underlying populations; to safeguard the United States as the centre of the international financial system; to maintain the United States (and, specially, US capitalists/corporations) in the top perch in the imperialist pecking order; and to prevent countries from breaking away from the system of global controls' – it is not enough to have a military bigger than that of any other power, it must be bigger than that of any plausible combination of other powers and this applies of course not only to immediate situation but to what might be the situation five or ten years from now, when the potential challenges of today might become real. It is pushing ahead with plans for a capability to fight two major regional conflicts at the same time.

The United States has the world's largest stockpile of weapons of mass destruction, chemical, biological and nuclear, and is the only state ever to have used the nuclear weapons. It is an arch votary of the unequal Nuclear Non-Proliferation Treaty and, even as it regularly arm-twists the minor nuclear nations, has refused to ratify the Comprehensive Nuclear Test Ban Treaty (CTBT). It has unilaterally withdrawn from the Anti-Ballistic Missile (ABM) Treaty and is busy developing weapons like the nuclear bunker-busting bombs. According to a classified Pentagon report the Bush administration has directed the military to prepare continency plans to use nuclear weapons against countries it sees as America's immediate or potential enemies, and to build new smaller nuclear weapons for use in certain battlefield situations. Despite objections from its European allies that it is unnecessary and will most likely trigger a new arms race, despite opposition of Russia and China, despite a protest by as many as 50 Nobel Laureates headed by Hans A. Bethe, one of the architects of the atom bomb, who have called it a 'wasteful' and 'dangerous' system, the National Missile Defence System remains a priority on the agenda of the United States. Its National Security Strategy, with its policy of military supremacy over the entire earth and the doctrine of pre-emption is nothing less than the declaration of a new imperial order to be backed up not only by the threat but also the aggressive, pre-emptive employment of overwhelming power against any country not to its liking. Most recently, following upon its yesterday's 'Star Wars Project' or the current 'Missile Defense System' argued for as 'defensive shields', though nothing of the kind– the United States has gone in for their heavily updated, blatantly offensive successor, codenamed 'Falcon'(Force Application and Launch from the Continental US) – its unmanned delivery vehicles, carrying a payload of 12.000 pounds and flying at speeds of up to 10 times the speed of sound will be able to strike targets 9.000 nautical miles distant in less than two hours. As John Pike, head of the Washington think tank. Global Security. Org has commented: 'It is about blowing people up on the other side of the planet even if no country on earth will allow us to use their territory'. The purpose, obviously, is to enable the US to go it alone against whichever country they please to subdue or destroy in their design to achieve world domination.

The global expansion of military power on the part of the hegemonic state of world capitalism is an integral part of economic globalisation. (The other advanced capitalist countries tied into the system are also reliant on the U.S. as the main enforcer of the rules of the game). The American ruling class knows that economics are ultimately a matter of politics, that it is relations of power, above all military power, that command the market, that there will be no 'global market' without an American military empire. 'The hidden hand of the market will never work without the hidden fist – McDonald's cannot flourish without McDonnell Douglas, the designer of the F-15. And the hidden fist that keeps the world safe for Silicon Valley's technologies is called the United States Army, Air Force, Navy and Marine Corps.' – this is how Thomas Friedman, who incidentally was also an adviser to Madeleine Albright, has put it in his article we have noticed earlier. Friedman goes on to quote approvingly from foreign policy historian Robert Kagan: 'Good ideas and technologies need a strong power that promotes those ideas by example and protects those ideas by winning on the battlefield. If a lesser power were promoting our ideas and technologies, they would not have the global currency that they have.'

Naturally, the hidden fist has to come out of hiding from time to time if it is going to make its point. And here the United has a long history. Monroe doctrine onwards it is a history of armed interventions or wars along with coercive diplomacy, bloody coups and covert actions against other sovereign states to make the world 'safe' for american business. In the half century since the World War II alone, on one pretext or another – 'containing communism' 'protecting American lives', 'punishing, "rogue", 'states', 'war on terrorism' or even 'promoting democracy', etc. – America has thus aggressed against countries as far afield as Greece and Cuba, Chile and Vietnam. Brazil, Guatemala and Dominican Republic, Grenada, Nicaragua, EL Salvador and Panama, Angola and Mozambique, Iran, Iraq, Libya and Afghanistan. And the list is far from complete. Here we may also notice that apart specific economic objectives or military gains, a most significant aspect of America's use of military force since the end of the Second World War – its important wars from Korea to the Balkans, the Gulf and Afghanistan – has been its political objectives: the 'containment' of external enemies or of internal opposition, diverting attention from tricky domestic problems or even the narrower political objectives of electoral advantage through displays of 'toughness' or tough 'nationalism'. That is how it needs to be noted that as a globalising power America's militarism does not generally have territorial ambitions, it does not seek direct physical control or hegemony over specific colonies. It is, typically, the use of massive displays of force to assert the dominance of global capital so that this capital, particularly the American segment of it, can freely navigate the global economy without hindrance. If at times it has the appearance of a naked display of imperial power for its own sake, without any specific or immediate objectives– and an outright military victory is neither an issue nor even a possible outcome – it is just to show who is boss, that is to make a general point about US domination of the world, its hegemony over global economy. As one comment has it, 'such display of imperial power only shows that US imperial hegemony can't now rely. if it ever could, on economic superiority alone, and that it depends on periodic display of sheer force. It hardly matters where or for what ostensible purpose, though it helps if the target is non-European or non-white.'

Beyond these economic, political and military aspects, a specific feature of the current situation is the ideological and cultural sweep of capitalist ideas and values that, in its own way, defines the current phase of globalization. Capitalism's technological ingenuity has made it possible for its principles to find their way into social, institutional and cultural spaces that even a few decades ago were beyond their reach. Commodity relations and moralities of the market are penetrating into every aspect of our lives, producing profit of course, but also ravaging morals and culture everywhere. A process of culture penetration is on – including what is described as 'McDonaldisation', 'the American way of life', 'homogenisation or leveling down of cultures', or simply as 'consumerist culture' – whereby the bourgeoisie today 'makes the world in its own image' with an immunity almost unparalleled since Marx wrote these words 150 odd years ago. This culture penetration is not just an extension but integral part of globalisation as imperialist domination. Imperialism has never been merely an economic-military system of control and exploitation. Cultural domination, an effort to penetrate and dominate the cultural life of the popular classes in order to reorder the values, behaviour, institutions and identity of the oppressed peoples to conform with the interests of the imperial classes, was always an integral part of it. So it is now with globalisation as a new, latest form of imperialism. Besides, there are now direct material benefits to be had, as never before. Recognising American economic and cultural domination in the on-going globalisation. James Petras has written:

> US cultural imperialism has two goals – one economic and the other political – to capture markets for its cultural commodities and to establish hegemony by shaping popular consciousness. The

> export of entertainment commodities is one of the most important sources of capital accumulation and global profits displacing manufacturing exports. In the political sphere, cultural imperialism plays a major role in dissociating people from their cultural roots and traditions of solidarity, replacing them with media created 'needs', which change with every publicity campaign. The political effect is to alienate people from traditional class and community bonds, atomising and separating individuals from each other.

(It may be mentioned that religious fundamentalism (especially the Islamic) so rampant today, is significant, partly at least, for its opposition to 'consumerism of the the west' or 'the American way of life', the imperialist cultural domination it is resourceless to understand or overcome. But it has acquired this significance primarily because the traditional Left alternatives, in particular the great revolutionary traditions of Marxism and communism seem to have become, for the time being at least, unavailable.)

To be particularly noticed is the ideological domination or hegemony that capitalism has come to acquire in the current phase of capitalist globalization. With capitalism become all but universal, it has also become ideologically hegemonic as never before. It is today so powerful and pervasive as to have become invisible, and is all the more powerful for being invisible. You no longer mention or recognize it or even refer to it by its proper name. It is 'globlisation', 'liberalisation', 'structural adjustment', 'economic reform', 'new economic policy' (and with the new votaries from the Left in India joining in) 'industrialisation', 'development and progress', even 'civilisation', etc. – that is anything but capitalism. A consensus on behalf of capitalism has emerged that makes it virtually immune against criticism or any discussion of alternatives (which, incidentally also makes nonsense of the much-vaunted pluralism of bourgeois democracy, gaining for it a spurious credibility only by a bizarre blowing up of minor differences among competitors in the politics of 'actually existing capitalism'). Given the collapsed Soviet regime's spurious identification with socialism, bourgeois ideologues have gone to town proclaiming the inevitability and virtues of capitalism. It is not only that the world is noisy with the refrain that 'there is no alternative', that the 'economic reforms' are 'irreversible' and that the world must adjust to the so-called rationality and efficiency requirements of 'the ecomomy', today every human practice, every social relationship, virtually everything under the sun including the natural environment is subject to the requirements of profit-maximisation. As Michael Lowy has noted:

> Indeed, never until the end of the 20th century has capital succeeded in exerting such a complete, absolute, undivided, and unlimited sway over the whole world. Never in the past has it had its current ability to impose its rules, its policies, its dogmas, and its interests upon all the nations of the globe. Never have international finance capital and multinational corporations been so out of control by states and peoples. Never before now has there existed such a dense network of international institutions– International Monetary Fund, World Bank, World Trade Organisation – devoted to controlling, governing, and administering human life according to the strict rules of the capitalist free market and unrestricted pursuit of capitalist profitability. Finally, never in any preceding epoch have all spheres of human life – social relationships, culture, art, politics, sexuality, health, education, sports, recreation – been so completely dominated by capital, so deeply submerged in 'the icy water of egotistical calculation.'

Underpinning this ideological domination are new information and communication technologies which have added immensely to the power of those in command of the mass media, advertisement and entertainment to control popular consciousness, to turn whole people, like individuals glued to their TV sets, into what the German poet Hans Magnus Enzensberger has called 'secondary illiterates', those who need neither memory nor any thinking or learning to sustain themselves. These are of little worth to them, the passive subjects in a world where the reigning ideology is consumerism with its exclusive concern for 'instant gratification' and 'contentment'. A market-driven 'mass culture' has come up which on the one hand aims at developing consumer instincts in the people to the utmost and thereby expanding markets for the greater glory of late-capitalist profit-making and, on the other hand, at ideological brainwashing of the people, diverting them from any advanced social ideals and implanting in their minds bland, illusory and often downright false and reactionary views of social and political realities.

A 'true idiot culture', Carl Bernstein has called it, where for the 'first time in history the weird and the stupid and the vulgar are becoming our cultural norm, even our cultural ideal'. Even as a 'stupid and vulgar' culture is mass purveyed via television screens, tabloid newspapers, glossy magazines and similar other means, the tendency is to pitch all messages to the lowest level of mental capacity. Knowledge is reduced to slick, pre-digrested, easy to understand capsules, inducing people to want simple answers to difficult problems. People's consciousness is transferred on to philistine, narrow-minded lines, and interest in truth which demands hard, complex and subtle exercise of mind, simply recedes into the background. The overall consequence is a dilution and dispersal of people's questioning spirit, their angry or combustible sentiments, an emasculation of their critical consciousness. There is general enervation of civil society, its . members rendered incapable of 'Answering back' as C. Wright Mills once phrased it. According to Jean Baudrillard, the very possibilities of critical examination and reflection are destroyed. In other words, the inundations of consumerism and 'mass culture' leave the alienated individuals of contemporary late-capitalist society eminently vulnerable to capitalism's hegemonic control. Though oppressed and exploited, they are now more open to 'colonisation of the mind' – victims internalisation of the cliche 'there is no alternative', their willing suspension of ideals and acceptance of a sub-autonomous existence in the interest of maintaining a secondary or even a tertiary position in the obtaining 'reality' – be it the capitalist society or for that matter the global capitalist system. For that is also what the 'third world mentality' is all about.

So much for 'globalisation' as the overall conditioning context of the Indian economic and political situation today.

Of this situation, the ruling class shift to 'globalisation' or 'economic reforms' as their strategic option, there are a few other aspects or implications which need to be taken note of.

To begin with, it is to be noted that prior to India's independence in 1947, state intervention in the economy was deemed necessary by the then economically and legitimacy-wise politically weak Indian bourgeoisie itself (cf. Bombay Plan, 1944). A major beneficiary of 'economic growth' during the Nehru era and afterwards, it soon developed substantial strength of its own and grew hopeful of new avenues of profit-making at home and abroad in partnership with global capitalism. The shift to globalisation, therefore, can be viewed as a natural progress for the Indian bourgeoisie, signalling a further consolidation of its position and power in the state.

Again, globalisation's shift to 'market economy' is usually justified by the bourgeois ideologues as a response to the failure of state intervention in the economy, more commonly the failure of the public sector. Now, apart from the fact that the public sector– which by itself has no *socialist* implications – has a successful presence in many capitalist economies and was a roaring success in the erstwhile 'socialist' countries, the public sector in India has not been the kind of failure bourgeois ideologues make it out to be. There are 'the stunning achievements of the National Thermal Power Corporation, Bharat Heavy Electricals, Nalco, the Oil and Natural Gas Commission, the Gas Authority of India or the Indian Oil Corporation' as a knowledgeable scholar has recently pointed out. And even the failure of public sector in India, such as it has been, is better understood as the failure of Indian democracy whence alone correctives to its malfunctioning or failure could have come, unlike the private sector where correctives come from the market, though often needing to be backed by the state. Therefore, the answer to this failure is a differently working democracy, an effective exercise of people's power in the state, and not a market-based private sector with its record of now well established worse failures.

It may be added that even otherwise Indian democracy is a rather sickly affair. That Indian democracy's failure to deliver has come to be raised to the status of a theory, indeed a 'law' of politics ('anti-incumbency', etc.) is as good an indication of the poor state of health of India's democracy and its 'democratic politics' as any other. It is a significant achievement of the ruling class politicians in India that, while their 'democratic politics;' has failed to deliver so far as the people are concerned, they have managed to give politics itself a dirty name and thus helped themselves and helped better secure their system against revolutionary politics as well. 'Politics is dirty business', the much-mouthed middle class protest is only seemigly radical. It leave the field all the more open for dirty politics, 'the politicians' politics' (*la politique politicienne*) as Malraux called it, and makes it that more difficult to develop an alternative 'people's politics'.

Yet again: that the shift to globalisation was unaccompanied by any debate or discussion, serious opposition or questioning, points, among other things, to the essential class character of the politics currently dominant in the country.

Marcuse has said somewhere that the success of a system is when it makes alternatives unthinkable. This is the success that capitalism achieved, or seemed to have achieved, in the aftermath of the Soviet collapse. The reality of capitalism catching up, the euphoria over this success is long over in most places. But, a Sainath may decry 'corporate hijack' of media agendas and a Bhikku Parekh may bemoan country's lack of 'an inspiring moral vision', capitalism's success is resonant in the 'silences' of the public discourse in India and in the Indian ruling elites' commitment to 'economic reforms'. Capitalism or 'market society' is taken for granted; for them it is the only possible mode of existence. Even as the reality of a third-worldist capitalism is painfully there all around us, not only is socialism forgotten (except for occasional denigration), even a discussion of capitalism is conspicuously absent. In the consensus built around the establishment ideology, to *think* capitalism remains decreed out of bounds. The Congress and the BJP share in this consensus and its ideology – a class ideology, it may be noted, is seldom, if ever, all of one piece; generally it is constituted by many ideas, doctrines, systems of dogma and philosophies which seemingly compete and even contradict each other but are socially supplementary. For the same reason, like the Congress, the BJP represents the interests of India's capitalist class and its allies, which representation is not a matter of class origin, background or membership in the class, or of personal inclinations or convictions but, as Marx put it, 'what makes them representatives (of the class) is the fact that in their minds they do not get beyond the limits which the latter do not get beyond in life, that they are consequently driven, theoretically, to the same problems and solutions to which material interest and social position drive the latter practically.' It is thus that the two parties, or their leaderships are unable to see beyond the limits postulated by the 'economic reforms'. The only economy they know is 'market economy'. The only possible form of development for them is capitalist development. The two are not that different as their leaders think or would have us believe. The differences between the two are important only at the tactical level. Strategically the BJP is as committed to 'economic reforms' as the Congress. That is why it is mistaken to see the BJP only as a communal party and that is how, while its opponents, including the Left, impotently locked themselves up in a 'communalism-secularism' trap, the BJP merrily went on implementing the Congress initiated 'economic reforms' whithout much notice or objection. As Radhika Desai, a Canadian scholar, has noted:

> The Indian capitalist class may be senior, practically venerable, among the bourgeoisies of the Third World, and it may have benefited from liberalising economic policies under practically every administration since the late 1970s. But the NDA governments presided over such a massive dose of the most brazen and unapologetic liberalisation as to constitute a virtual rebirth of the capitalist class, sired by the BJP. Indian capitalists' new filial loyalty cannot be underestimated. The NDA oversaw a vast and ungrudging expansion of practically every sector of the urban industrial economy: finance and financial markets, the media, housing and construction, consumer durables and non-durables of every kind. Privatisation was accelerated, giving a great fillip to the stock markets; the foreign exchange regime was further liberalised; FDI and portfolio investments, including by foreign institutional investors, FIIs, flowed in. Consumer credit to finance lifestyles of intemational standards (indeed, better, thanks to the cheapness of domestic labour) for a small but very visible stratum of those in business and professions was expanded and liberalised, as was the import regime. The tax burden on the rich was reduced; innumerable small quotas and restrictions on economic activity were lifted; the IT sector boomed, exploying thousands of young professionals and arousing unprecedented hopes of upward mobility among thousands of others; and, not least, the objective of closer ties between India and its wealthy 'diaspora' in the metropoles was pursued by taking the first steps towards granting dual citizenship. All talk of the poor and of larger social goals was dismissed routinely as the leftover cant of yesterday's 'licence-permit raj'. It was truly a dream government for the possessing classes.

Needless to say, the effect of these measures on the whole economy was less than spectacular and, on the poor majority, positively disastrous. More than ever, the NDA governments created two nations in India, already home to some of the starkest divides between poverty and wealth. Every criticism from the Left had its counterpart in appreciation on the part of the rich, and there is no doubt about a feel-good factor among the propertied elite and foreign interests in India: in fact, an overwhelming pro-BJP sentiment.

This, of course, cost the BJP the 2004 Lok Sabha election. But it was no 'rout' as the opponents' wishful thinking tended to view it (the BJP's tally wa 136 seats to 145 for the Congress). The corporate world, happy over the BJP's performance in power, are desperately hopeful about its future as a 'modern' political party, alternating with the Congress in the much longed-for two-party system in India's parliamentary democracy. The corporates can well do with its *Hindutva* and the accompanying obscurantism. Capitalism needs science and technology, but, as we know from history, capitalist classes have always needed religion and obscurantism too. The BJP's aggressive nationalist posture could well be an advantage in the harsh competitive world of global economy and politics.

Finally, globalisation's shift to market economy has its obvious implications for the future of democracy in India. It is not surprising that its pursuit of the new strategic option, the so-called 'economic reforms', had the consequence of the Congress losing its credibility with the people and power to the BJP led NDA. The NDA Government, now pursued the same 'economic reforms' agenda, necessarily producing, in the words of Radhika Desai, 'a feel good factor among the propertied elite and foreign interests in India' and creating 'more than ever... two nations in India, already home to some of the starkest divides between poverty and wealth'. It was 'India shining', but only for a few at the top, with the many below experiencing its structurally *other* reality. Again, it was not suprising that the BJP lost the 2004 Lok Sabha election and its power at Delhi. Back in power on the *aam aadmi* plank, compulsions of electoral politics forcing it to take note of the victim of 'economic reforms', the so-called *aam aadmi* ('the common man'), the Congress now again speaks the Nehruvian language of economic growth with equity and social justice, etc. – a Manmohan-Sonia farce, as it were, to Nehru's tragedy, to paraphrase Marx's famous observation on the caricatured re-appearance of historical phenomenon.* The Congress now seeks 'economic reforms with a human face', something which, symbolic gestures apart – already forced on it by the supporting Left – 'economic reforms', because of its structural logic, simply cannot deliver – and this puts it at odds with democracy in India. In other words, while some muddling along for sometime is always possible, the structural nature of things being what it is, 'economic reforms' and democracy simply don't go together. I do not have to spell out the negative implications.

(It will not be out of place to mention here that the current long-term crisis of global capitalism has compelled it to shed its 'human face' even in the advanced capitalist West – dismantling, or struggle over dismantling the welfare state has been a distinct feature of economy and politics in the advanced capitalist countries in recent decades. A return to normal or typical capitalism, as we have already noted, is in fact a major aspect of capital's current phase of globalisation as against the welfarist capitalism of the earlier period which was really a conjunctural aberration in capitalism's long history as an exploitative system.)

Similar is the case with another of our cherished values, secularism, which is integral to India's survival as a democratic polity. If 'economic reforms' and democracy do not go together, 'economic reforms' and secularism too do not in the sense that in its failure to deliver, 'the economic reforms' regularly generates a basis for anti-secular developments. The shift to market economy has been accompanied or followed by the rise to prominence of the utterly reactionary, semi-fascist *Hindutva* ideology and politics, spelling its own disasters for the present and future

* This is how it goes in the opening para of Marx's *The Eighteenth Brumaire of Louis Bonaparte*: 'Hegel remarks somewhere that all facts and personages of great importance in world history occur, as it were, twice. He forgot to add: the first time as tragedy, the second as farce.'

of the Indian people. Here it needs to be understood that *'Hindutva'* has come up because our society today provides a continuing social-material basis for the production and reproduction, the rise, sustenance and spread of such ideas or ideologies. One does not have to be a Marxist to understand or recognise this. A long time ago, suggesting that ideas do not rise and prosper through some inherent power of their own, Herbert Spencer had said: 'ideas wholly foreign to social state cannot be evolved, and if introduced from without, cannot get accepted, or if accepted die out.' It is the economic, political and moral wreckage left behind by the failure of the Nehruvian project which has provided the 'social state', that is, the necessary social-meterial basis for the rise and growing acceptance of *'Hindutva'* as religious fundamentalism and a fascistic political ideology. 'Globalisation' or the so-called 'economic reforms', in its economic, political and moral-cultural consequences is daily piling up more such wreckage, creating more social-material basis for all sorts of fundamentalism, regressive ideologies and disintegrative politics. That is how the decade of the most vigorous debate over the issue of communalism and equally vigorous advocacy of secularism, the 1990s, was also the decade of the most heinous anti-secular developments and the BJP's rise to power at Delhi. One may well hazard the view that with the globalisation that is on, communalism and its consequences may well be a specific feature of the barbaric situation in India as part of the universal barbarism that capitalism now threatens the world with. That is, if the people do not effectively intervene, and do so in time, with ideology and politics, a strategic alternative, of their own.

•

The ruling classes of India have through their different political formations, decided to 'secede' from the people and opted for 'globalisation' as their strategic option for the future. The Indian people yet again face the question, whose full implications were somewhat obscured in 1947 due largely to the interim successes of the Soviet Union: what do they do in the current situation of global domination of capitalism? The historical experience in India and elsewhere in the Third World makes it abundantly clear that development which can meet the needs of our people is impossible within the framework of capitalism, national or globalised. Socialism has to be the strategic goal, whatever be the long or short transitional route to it.* Historical experience indeed allows no other choice.

This, however, is not to posit socialism as achievable today or tomorrow, or even the day after, but to posit it as people's alternative strategic goal, as the principle governing people's politics which links together their immediate, ongoing and emerging struggles in an ultimate project of revolutionary transformation of society, as the goal of a long transitional process whose specifics and speed will depend on the objective material conditions and the nature and balance of class forces involved at each stage of the struggle for the socialist goal. Immediately it means saying 'no' to globalisation, a 'delinking' from the global capitalist market, and opting for a pro-people socialism oriented autonomous development.

To say 'no' to globalisation is not to argue for any kind of 'autarky' in economic development. Essentially, it is a question of control over what a country produces and what it buys and sells abroad, the terms on which it does business with foreigners and engages in international exchange. More precisely, it is to pose the issue of this development being governed by *external* imperatives, those issuing from the requirements of the world capitalist market (export-led growth, etc.) and the associated consumerism of the rich, or primarily by *internal* imperatives, those flowing from an

* A mentioned earlier, it is socialism not as they built it in the erstwhile Soviet Union but as visualized by its classical tradition: a humane, democratically functioning society providing a superior and advanced form of freedom and self-determination to the people.

assessment of own resources and the needs of the people. Of course any attempt at saying 'no' to globalisation or 'delinking' is likely to exact a heavy price in many ways, including an unavoidable trade-off between the requrements of productivity and those of minimising the polarising impact of global capitalism's enormous economic power. But once 'productivism' is abandoned and human welfare has the priority, this need not be a deterrent to adopting the strategy that 'delinking' involves. This strategy, it may be added, is born of the historical experience that the more an economy is part of the international network of capitalist trade and finance, the more it becomes dependent on it, the more its domestic economy must adapt to the world price system, the requirements of international finance (including the discipline imposed by the International Monetary Fund) and the capitalist business cycle, with the result that the constraints of the world market become a dominant influence and the country so involved increasingly loses control over its own destiny. It may be further added that systemically anti-capitalist nature and direction of economic development is central to the strategy I am arguing for. Otherwise saying 'no' to globalisation, or 'delinking', may well get reduced to an argument for one or the other kind of *national* capitalist development which has already failed to deliver so far as the people's interests are concerned.

The stategy being advocated postulates an effective exercise of people's power in the state, with the state, truly committed to peoples's welfare, undertaking at the very outset a comprehensive programme of eradication of mass poverty, universal primary education, health care, housing, and provision of basic necessities for all. Initiating steps towards redistribution of incomes and development of backward areas will be a priority for state's active intervention in the economy which even as it covers such areas as foreign relations, production and social distribution, research and training, and the like, will need to secure an effective transitional combination of planning and market forces without letting the market or its values take over. Agrarian revolution benefiting the rural proletariat and small farmers, thereby improving the productive capacity in the rural areas, and layng the basis of cooperative effort and voluntary collectivisation of agriculture should be high on its agenda of economic reconstruction, as should be the transformation of the informal sector into a popularly managed transitional economy. A building up or restructuring of industry is obviously necessary. But it can neither be one based on 'international competitiveness' (that is promoting exports through low costs of local labour) nor on 'import substitution' (promoting production for the consumption of the privileged local classes). Not that all effort in these directions is ruled out; some of it may even be necessary. Only priorities, for years to come, lie elsewhere. Important thing is to develop and organise productive forces in a manner that helps the rural sector leap forward, carries industrialisation to the countryside and in general ensures a pattern of growth which, refusing the wasteful production to satisfy elite consumerism, immediately benefits the popular masses, satisfying their basic needs, needs created and satisfiable by the redistribution of income. It should be obvious that the overall development of our third world country today cannot support the first world consumption levels of our elites. What is needed is a diversification and development of internal makets for domestic goods and services governed by the overall principle that, beyond a certain necessary priority charges of an unequal nature, private needs and wants should be satisfied (and this goes for their increasing satisfaction) only at a level at which they can be satisfied for all, and beyond this all increase in the production of consumer goods should be for collective consumption.

What the above strategy in effect demands is that not economics or 'the market' but politics, that is people's politics, is put in command of the economy. 'Politics in command' means posing such questions as: growth? but which growth? for what purpose? for whose sake, whose benefit or profit? for what kind of society and within which environment? Are social needs the guide or the market and its profit-making? Is it to get the maximum welfare of all the people, with priority for the needs of the poorest sections and the most backwards regions and for the protection of environment? Or is to satisfy the market-induced, ecologically unsustainable consumerist hunger of the privileged part of the population seeking to maintain or attain the 'high' living standards of the west? These are questions which are central to any search for a real alternative to capitalism. We must ask: is our goal meeting 'the needs of the economy', its 'anonymous masters' as they have been called – 'abstractions such as financial markets, interest rates, exchange rates, commodity prices, indexes and statistical artefacts of all kinds'– or satisfaction of the needs of the people, allowing citizens the possibility of living as human beings? Is the starting point of our economic exercises to be calculation of deficits in order to cut them at the cost of the people or a determination of resources needed to satisfy people's needs in order to find or raise them? And our language? Do we practice the obscurantism of GDP, fiscal and revenue deficits, balance of payments, growth rates etc, or speak more humanely in terms of such things as food and clean drinking water, health care and sanitation, housing and education and the like so that economy becomes a transparent and accountable means of integrating these basic human needs of the people with a planned use of domestic resources, an use which also takes care of questions of equality, social justice including gender justice, employment, ecologically sustainable development, and so on.

Such a socialism-oriented pro-people autonomous development process will draw on own strengths and domestic resources and capacities, including those of the hardworking poor who yet remain the most creative and productive force in our society. It will give our common people, an overwhelming mass of workers and peasants, a positive stake in the economy and mobilise them for building a better society as well as for the inevitable struggle against global imperialism and its local allies or partners – an awakened and aroused people are indeed the best defence even against armed aggression. Needless to add, such popular mobilisation and struggle will be all the time necessary to carry through the strategic option that socialism-oriented delinking and development involve.

Economic and technological backwardness is often pressed as an argument to counter the plea for such autonomous economic development. (Getting access to the most modern technology is another usual argument for the need to actively participate in world trade). Here, apart from the fact that in India we are not that lacking in technology or the talent for it, two brief observations are in order. In the first place it is useful to recognise that if, despite economic backwardness, priority is given to the needs of the poorest and most deprived sections of the people, there is much that can be done at the outset even in the absence of growth of productive forces. The redistribution of wealth and the use of idle or under-utilised human and material resources, their more productive deployment, can bring quick improvement in health, education and general living conditions of large masses of people. Early years of post-revolutionary sociaties in the Soviet Union and elsewhere provide ample evidence of this achievement which could be the basis for further development along socialist lines.

In the second place, once we overcome the fetishism of science and technology – which (as, for example, with Nehru's 'temples of modern India', etc.) attributes to them properties or power they do not possess, and at times even expects them to do the job of a social revolution which they cannot – and, as with economic development, so with technology, ask the basic question: 'technology for what purpose?', the argument for getting access to the most modern western technology via globalisation – even if that was certain which it most certainly is not – loses much of its force. If the purpose is to satisfy the consumerist hunger of the privileged part of the population and therefore supply it with the most modern gadgets, designs, and goodies of the west, then rushing into globalisation is indeed understandable. But if the purpose or priority is to meet the needs of all the people for decent food, clothing and shelter, clean water, proper sanitation and health protection, education and cultural opportunities and the like, then devoting scarce resources to the most modern technology will only be wasteful because there is little in the latest technology of the west that would make a significant contribution. In fact what is most useful and relevant in technology, western or otherwise, for improving the way of life of the masses is widely known. Most of this technology is already available at home and what else is needed is obtainable in the normal course of managed trade...

'Politics incommand', that is, a socialism-oriented development really involves making a fundamental and principled choice, namely, divorcing the criteria of rationality in economic-social life from those that govern the market-based system of capitalism. 'Delinking' is making a similar choice in relation to global capitalism. No autarky, it is yet reversing the process of peripheral 'adjustment' to global capitalism, that is subordinating external relations to the logic of socialism-directed internal development. Instead of our country adjusting its internal agendas to the world expansion of capitalism, to the imperatives of the global (capitalist) market, it is the imperatives of internal socialism-oriented development which must have the primacy. It may be specifically noted that these imperatives reject the SEZ path to industrialisation or economic growth which subjects our poor peasantry to the savagery of a modern-day 'primitive accumulation of capital'. Instead, the socialist perspective here, which was also the perspective of Marx, Lenin and Mao, is thus stated by Engels:

> What, then, is our attitude towards the small peasantry? How shall we have to deal with it on the day of our accession to power?...we foresee the inevitable doom of the small peasant, but... it is not our mission to hasten it by any interference on our part...
>
> ..., it is just as evident that when we are in possession of state power, we shall not even think of forcibly expropriating the small peasants (regardless of whether with or without compensation), as we shall have to do in the case of the big landowners. Our task relative to the small peasant consists, in the first place, in effecting a transition of his private enterprise and private possession to cooperative ones, not forcibly but by dint of example and the proffer of social assistance for this purpose...
>
> We, of course, are decidely, on the side of the small peasant, we shall do everything at all permissible to make his lot more bearable, to facilitate his transition to the cooperative should he decide to do so, and even to make it possible for him to remain on his small holding for a protracted length of time to think the matter over, should he still be unable to bring himself to this decision.
>
> We do this not only because we consider the small peasant living by his own labour as virtually belonging to us, but also in the direct interest of the Party. The greater the number of peasants whom we can save from being actually hurled down into the proletariat, whom we can win to our side while they are still peasants, the more quickly and easily the social transformation will be accomplished.

•

Finally a few words about this thing called 'development' and the issues it raises. Now, the concept of 'development' is by nature ideological in the sense that it is suggestive of something desirable, which obviously implies that it is not necessarily synonymous with capitalist development, that the people are free to reject the latter, its 'way of the market', as undesirable. Incidentally, the currently fashionable neo-liberal argument about the inseparability of 'democracy' and 'market' as two fundamental requirements in a modern society is self-contradictory. If there is democracy then it is up to the people to determine whether or not (and to what extent) to use markets. It would be contradictory to leave the choice of institutions to the people and at the same time to pre-close that choice by insisting that the market form of organisation be, in fact, chosen. As Amartya Sen has put it: 'if democracy is to be an irresistable force then the market system cannot be an immovable object'. (And, it may be added that in the history of capitalism, market systems have cohabited most comfortably with dictatorial regimes).

Again, that the initial modern economic and industrial development, that in the west, occurred in the capitalist form is no reason to assume that this is the only way it can take place. The man who best studied and theorised this development certainly did not think so. Marx was categorical in rejecting the idea that this was the path 'every people is fated to tread.' He infact regarded the capitalist path, the path of market-governed economic development, as simply unworthy of human beings. Hence his argument for socialism, foı people 'rationally, regulating their interchange with nature' in a manner 'worthy of their human nature'.

If needs to be noted that the issue here is not market but '*capitalist* market', that is the degree to which the market guides the flow of investment or is used as an independent regulator of economy. The key question, in other words, is : who controls the surplus, and how it is used? in pursuit of profit or to serve human needs? Important here is the crucial distinction between market exchange and market forces. A market will be needed in a socialism-oriented economy, but not 'market forces'. Thus, for example, about one kind, or use, of the market at least there should be little if any dispute. Under capitalism, however modified by history, state intervention, etc., market has three particularly important functions: it serves as a mechanism for allocating productive resources among various uses, as a way of deciding how much individuals and groups get paid for their labour or other assets they own, and as a means of distributing goods and services to consumers. In a socialism-oriented planned economy, while the first two functions, for the most part, and again with due modifications, would be performed through democratic planning which would determine the priorities of economic development and human welfare, the third can be for the most part entrusted to the market. A market would be needed and useful for distributing most goods and services to consumers. This apart, subject to the basic purposes of the socialism-oriented economy sought to be realised through democratic planning, market can be used as a tool for operationalising the plan: in facilitating the overall responsiveness of the economy; in serving notice of people's needs or preferences, and of their relative strength by the direct pressure of supply and demand and thus ensuring, quantity and quality-wie, better distribution of goods and services; in providing an accurate idea of the costs of what is produced, though this will not govern the pricing policies; in economic accounting of the individual and collective participants in the economy; in helping check the overall adequacy and rationality of planning and providing indicators to monitor optimisation, and so on.

In other words, certain instruments and institutions now associated with the market can indeed be necessary and useful in a socialism-oriented economy, but the moving force of the economy has to emanate not from the market but from democratic planning which, replacing the rationality of the market as the driving mechanism, ensures that the benefits of this replacement accrue not to workers alone but to people as a whole, benefits ranging from the terms and conditions of work and leisure to their larger implications for the quality of social life, culture, the environment, and in general those 'non-economic' or 'extra-economic' goods which, according to Marx, make for a truly rich human existence.

That such, non-capitalist, socialism-oriented path of development is both desirable and possible is more than validated by the Soviet experiment in socialism. What was ultimately built in the Soviet Union was a very much deformed socialism – deformed partly at least by its 'productivist' push to catch up with capitalism rather than build up socialist relations in the economy. The failures of central planning under the 'actually existing socialism' — as we had come to call it– especially during its last decades, are also now universally understood – chief among these failures being the way in which the lack of democracy engendered an all-powerful stifling bureaucracy so that the central premises of socialism were, time and again, debauched. Yet it bears asserting that flawed in its planning or deformed otherwise, socialism-oriented economy in the Soviet Union had great and in some cases truly astonishing achievements to its credit, without parallel in the historyof capitalist development anywhere in the world and all the more significant because of the surrounding circumstances, particularly the starting point of extreme backwardness, made worse by the ruination of the first world war and a civil war, and later, having to begin from the scratch again after the second world war, along with a totally hostile international environment, globally dominant capitalism's constant pressure of hot and cold war, throughout its troubled history. Its prodigies of industrialization in the thirties constitute an incontrovertible argument for the capacity of a planned socialism-oriented economy to achieve growth – in a single decade it turned the country into the world's second industrial power and created the powerful Soviet state that survived years of capitalist hostility and encirclement and could take on the full might of world fascism and defeat it, an argument well confirmed by the spectacular performance of the Soviets during the years of reconstruction immediately following the Second World War when, with more than 20 million dead, its lands revaged and economy wrecked by war, rejecting all imperialist aid, through its own planned self-reliant effort, the country was rebuilt into the world's other super-power. (Incidentally in the midst of the Great

Depression of the 1930s which brought even the strongest of capitalist economies to its knees, the Soviet Union not only remained immune to this global crisis but recorded exceptional of economic advance.) Beyond economy, there are other, even more significant, Soviet achievements. So far as the common people are concerned, in terms of employment, which is the very basis of dignity and hope in society, in terms of nutrition, health care, education, housing etc., items that consume 60 to 80 per cent of a family budget in most capitalist societies, Soviet Union had done decidedly better than capitalism has. In fact, in terms of quality of life in general, of how economy affects the everyday life and well-being of the common man, the Soviet achievement remains unprecedented, Soviet socialism provided full employment and secure jobs, a modest scale of income and consumption for all even if it lacked west's consumerist affluence. It guaranteed cradle to grave social security with health care, education, housing or transport within every one's easy reach. It ensured stable prices throughout its seventy odd years of existence. Supply of housing offered at unbelievably low rates may have lagged behind demand, but there were no extensive shanty towns in the Soviet Union. Nor did one ever see an old person begging in its streets. Soviet Union had by far the highest ratio of doctors (and hospital beds) to population of any large or even medium-sized capitalist country. It had the best infant and child care in the world. Soviet socialism indeed took care, in fact loving care, of old men and women and children. Even in the remotest villages and most backward republics of the Soviet-Union, socialism connoted universal literacy and health care and a greatly enhanced status for women. Women, throughout Soviet Union won levels of participation not seen before. They mass advanced into the professions earlier than any other country and remained statistically far ahead of the west. To the universally recognised educational achievement of socialism we may add widespread promotion of sports. It used to happen almost as a matter of course that two-thirds of the Olympic medals came to be won by young men and women from the socialist world. Socialism in the Soviet Union also meant huge subsidisation of literature, music and arts, and the diffusion of classical world culture on a mass-scale, unprecedented in any major country of the world, including the US, Germany and Japan, symbolised by the selling of hundreds of millions of copies of Shakespeare, Tolstoy, Pushkin, Gorki and Tagore and discs of Beethoven and Bach at throw away prices, or distribution of Bolshoi Ballet tickets among the workers. To which may be added across-the board resuscitation of people's art, music and dance forms in the vast stretches of Central Asian republics quite apart from the pinnacles of achievement the Bolshoi and Kirov Ballet groups attained with direct encouragement from the Soviet authorities. Even if we choose to ignore the significance of the exceedingly short time within which all this was accomplished or the fact that it was accomplished while achieving a balance in military strength with the world's most powerful nation, the United States, socialism as it existed in the Soviet Union represents a social and cultural achievement that is unparalleled anywhere in the advanced capitalist world.

Such was the overall achievement in the Soviet Union that it was hailed as *a new civilisation*. Sidney and Beatrice Webb's monumental study, *Soviet Communism : A New Civilisation*, is at once a recognition of and a tribute to what the revolution-inspired Soviet people and communists had achieved, as they pioneered the path to socialism.

Looked at in narrow economistic terms, what this achievement involved was a socialism-oriented politicisation of the surplus utilisation process as against the profit driven surplus utilisation process of a 'market economy'. Of course, as I am going to argue, this achievement has to be dissociated from the authoritarian or dictatorial system it came associated with. Planning that a socialism-oriented economy necessarily demands has to be democratic. It has been rightly argued that with democracy the Soviet achievement would have been not only more impressive but lasting as well. These consideration, I may add, point to the 'doing something new' that socialism-oriented path of development entails.

•

The current crisis of global capitalism with its scams and scandals and the worldwide devastation it has caused, only strengthens our argument for a non-capitalist, socialism-oriented path of development. This crisis has simultaneously exposed globalisation's reality as capitalism and the crisis-ridden reality of capitalism, whose nature and consequences Marx had so brilliantly analysed 150 odd years ago. It was part of Marx's critique of capitalism that while transition from feudalism to capitalism represented a tremendous advance towards a more rational condition of humankind, the inherent irrationality of capitalism as a system of private property and profit-driven market economy would warp and hinder further economic and social progress. Hence the transitory character of capitalism. The structural logic of capitalism, its accumulation process generating wealth and poverty at opposite poles, inevitably leads to recurring crises of over production – people's purchasing power again and again failing to match the increasing production that capitalists put in the market. Marx saw these crises as an expression of 'the revolt of modern production forces against the property elations that are the conditions for the existence of the bourgeoisie and its rule', and therefore indicative of the need to overcome and abolish these property relations to make possible production geared not to profit in the marketplace, but to satisfaction of people's needs. It may be added that 'crisis of over production' or 'excess capacity' has been a perennial tendency in capitalism. Such slumps or crises at regular intervals have been a charactristic feature of capitalist development, from at least 1825 on, with capitalism's internal mechanisms becoming increasingly inadequate to cope with them, making it necessary for the capitalist state to intervene to save capitalism— save it, as it were, from the capitalists themselves. So it has been throughout, notably at the time of the Great Depression of the 1930s and so it is now. The specificities involved in its occurrence notwithstanding, as in the case of the Great Depression, the current crisis is an expression of the inherent irrationality of capitalism, of its structural logic. Incidentally, there is an interesting aspect to the similarity between the Great Depression and the current crisis. The usual post-war boom or the cyclical upswing of the 1920s, coming as it in the context of the October Revolution, had promoted a debate over *Ford versus Marx,* with the bourgeois ideologues glaeefully proclaiming victory to Ford. The glee however was short-lived. The old contradiction soon resurfaced to haunt capitalism – the stock markets crashed and the Great Depression was on. Much the same has happened today. For decades, especially after the collapse of Soviet socialism, we had the bourgeois ideologues celebrating the 'trimph of capitalism,' proclaiming the virtues of neo-liberalism and its free market and affirming (even believing) that crisis-ridden capitalism, its mass unemployment etc. were things of the past. But the logic of the *capitalist* market has again asserted itself — the stock markets have crashed and another global crisis of capitalism is on. One reacalls Sweezy and Magdoff's response to the post-Soviet capitalist triumphalism. They had written: 'Capitalism's victory settles nothing. In its global form, it encompasses ever more people and intensifies their exploitation and oppression. History shows that there have been alternatives in the past, and reason tells us that there will be other in the future...'

The current crisis, it bears repeating, is not something accidental, a result of irresponsibilities of the banking system or of some mistaken neo-liberal policies. Nor is it 'a crisis of globalisation', whatever that means. Instead, it is a systemic, structural crisis of capitalism, a crisis *of* the system and not just a crisis *in* the system. I may here quote two passages from my *Crisis of Socialism – Notes in Defence of a Commitment (written in 2004):*

> ... it is capitalism's deep-seated tendency to generate more surplus than it can absorb. As contemporary monopoly capitalism, it carries a contradiction within itself; on the one hand it generates a swelling flow of profits, on the other it reduces the demand for additional investment in increasingly controlled market: more and more profits, fewer and fewer profitable investment opportunities, with the consequence that capital accumulation and therefore economic growth which is powered by capital accumulation slows down. There is growing stagnation in the economy and a consequent augmentation of the role of finance in it. We have earlier noticed the double process of faltering real investment and burgeoning financialisation – a growing tendency for profits that could not find profitable outlets in real capital formation to be diverted into purely financial and mostly speculative channels – at the time of the Great Depression. Now with the intensified crisis of overproduction in the real economy we are faced with a similar but worse situation, indeed a 'financial explosion' – the vast expansion of debt, credit, and monetary and financial markets, extending from the Wall Street to the third world – as capital, facing stagnation within production, seeks alternative outlets for itself. There is a new,intensified manifestation of the tendency of capital to direct itself not so much towards making useful goods and services as towards manipulating money and speculation, making money directly without the intermediation of a production process. This has counteracted stagnation to some extent but spelled greater and greater instability in the economy as the system takes on an increasingly speculative character. The problem is not confined to the advanced capitalist countries but extends in various ways through the medium of imperialism to the periphery itself. A manifestation of the crisis of global capitalism, it has been exploding as a financial cataclysm in country after country with a regularity which has ceased to surprise – in Mexico (end of 1994), Brazil (1995), South Africa (1996), Eastern Europe (early 1997), Southeast Asia (late 1997), South Korea (early 1998), Russia and South Africa again (mid-1998), Brazil again (1998-1999) and Argentina soon after... Pundits are no longer asking if another country will be next, but who will be next.

Again:

> Quintessentially a system of capital accumulation, capitalism accumulates through regular generation of additional profit in the real economy, the one which produces goods and services that enable people to live and reproduce. But the very structure that yields these profits to capitalists puts strict limits on the incomes, and therfore purchasing power, of the underlying population. They are barely able to buy what has been produced – goods remain unsold and excess capacity comes to mark the economy. There is therefore no profit to be made from expanding the capacity to produce the goods that enter into mass consumption. To do so would be to invest in excess capacity, a patent capitalist irrationality. What then are capitalists to do with their profits? This is a problem which has dogged capitalism throughout its history. During its period of ascendancy, as capitalism grew and expanded at home and abroad, even as it regularly produced excess capacity and ran into crises of overproduction, new opportunities continued to become available for profitable investment in real productive assets. With capitalism becoming increasingly, and now truly, global, such opportunities have become scarce. Investment in financial assets has been capitalism's answer to its old problem. The process began with the stagnation of the 1970s and accelerated during the following decades, with the consequence that the old structure of the economy, consisting of a production system served by a more or less important financial adjunct now stands replaced by a new structure in which a vastly expanded financial section has achieved a high degree of independence and sits on top of the underlying production system. The capital accumulation process has come to be preeminently financialised. One consequence is that capital, no longer able to sustain maximum profitability by means of commensurate economic growth, has come to rely more and more on simply redistributing wealth in favour of the rich, and on increasing inequalities, within and between national economies with the help of the 'neoliberal state'. The other consequence is that cut loose from its origin and moorings in a real economy of production, financial capital has, almost inevitably, become speculative capital geared solely to its own expansion, accompanied equally inevitably by all sorts of speculative frauds and manipulation of financial institutions. A long time ago, with the experiences of the 1920s and 1930s in mind, Keynes had warned: 'speculators may

> do no harm as bubbles on a steady stream of enterprise. But the position is serious when enterprise becomes the bubble on a whirlpool of speculation. When the capital development of a country becomes a by-product of the activities of a casino, the job is likely to be ill-done.' Not only has the warning come true – the speculative bubble has so expanded on top of the economy that productive enterprise is very near being a 'bubble on the whirlpool of speculation' – the bubble, reflecting a serious contradiction at the heart of contemporary capitalism, the disconnection between the productive base of the economy and the financial superstructure, has been regularly bursting in one... country after another, devastating the lives of the peoples concerned and garnering new gains in capital and assets for the plundering multinationals. Such is the reality of capitalism today. Its dire consequences for the people are visible on all sides, from mass unemployment in the advanced capitalist countries to deepening poverty and destitution in the third world and unchecked ecological deterioration everywhere. But the point to be noticed in the immediate context is that the financialisation of capital accumulation distorts and negates what is the ultimate purpose of any economic system, the satisfaction of human needs – which puts an additional question mark over capitalism's legitimacy as an economic system for our times.

As in the past, bailed out by the state at the cost of the common people, capitalism will survive this crisis too – but only to get into deeper crises in the future. That is, in the absence of a successful challenge, capitalism may continue to survive in a state of 'depressed continuum', as Meszaros has called it, which also means capitalism's survival as a failed system. As I have written elsewhere:

> ...at the end of its five centuries old existence, global capitalism is a very much failed system today. The evidence of this failure is starkly visible in every part and aspect of contemporary capitalist world. It is visible in the impoverishment and immiseration on the rise just about everywhere in the world; in the official statistics on rates of unemployment, poverty, homelessness, and hunger; in the sullen slums of major cities of Western bourgeois democracies, proliferating urban ghettos of the grittly capitals of former Soviet bloc countries and the warrens of teeming tumble down shanties of the peripheral South; in the gross inequalities of

> the world, the wretchedness of the impoverished and excluded within the rich Western societies and the huge mass of misery in the poorer countries; in the morally intolerable and socially unnecessary suffering – what Bourdieu has called *la misere du monde* – produced by capitalism everywhere...

Again:

> The 'actually existing socialism'– which was not Marx's socialism whose possibility remains open – has of course, failed. But, surely, the 'actually existing capitalism' – which is the only kind of capitalism possible – has not been the success it is made out to be. In any objective judgement, capitalism too has been a failure in our times. Other considerations apart, capitalism has been a failure, in terms of possibly the most legitimate criteria for assessing the performance of a social system: 'fullness of employment' and 'goodness of employment' of the actual and potential resources available in society. Never before in human history has the gap between society's potentiality and society's performance been so immense as it is today in capitalism's current stage of development. Evidence is there in the extraordinary productive capacity that three successive industrial revolutions have put at the disposal of humankind and the poverty and illiteracy, squalid slums and homelessness that are the lot of millions of families in the wealthiest countries of the capitalist world and the hunger and misery of hundreds of millions of people, living out their emply and barren lives in the hovels of the peripheral or semi-peripheral poor countries of the third world. The third world today is indeed a monument to the failure of capitalism in our times...

This, however, is not to suggest any collapse of capitalism, now or in the future. Systems dont collapse like that. (Possibly the only exception in our times is the system in the Soviet Union which indeed 'self-destructed', something explained by the *sui generis* nature of the class exploitative system that the deformed Soviet socialism had ultimately degenerated into.) In other words, crisis or failure as mentioned above, is not to be confused with any so-called 'breakdown' or 'impending breakdown'. Capitalism will not collapse by itself. A nuclear war or a environmental disaster may lead to barbarism or worse. Otherwise the rule of capital will end when it is overthrown by the people. Hence uncertainties of the situation notwithstanding, the need is for socialists to put class struggle at the centre of their politics. And to be truly anti-systemic, it has to be a struggle for both reform and revolution with the former subordinated to the latter as enjoined by Marx. 'An anti-systemic movement,' as Wallerstein has argued, 'cannot neglect short term defensive action, including electoral action. The world's populations live in the present, and their immediate needs have to be addressed. Any movement that neglects them is bound to lose the widespread passive support that is essential for its long-term success. But the motive and justification for defensive action should not be that of remedying a failing system...' Apart from seeking to prevent the systems negative effect from getting worse in the short run, defensive action (or the struggle for reform) should be so conducted as to subserve the long-term revolutionary aim of a transcedence of the system itself.

•

In positing socialism as the strategic goal and setting socialism-oriented development as the agenda to reach this goal, it helps to take a look at Marx's own perspective in the matter and the altered reality of the world today.

Socialism, as we know, arose in opposition to capitalism with the rise of modern capitalism itself. Marx's many-sided critique of capitalism soon provided it with a scientific theoretical basis, establishing it as socialism of our times, distinguishing it from its various other forms – some of which (Reactionary Socialism, Petty-bourgeois Socialism, German or 'True' Socialism, Conservative or Bourgeois Socialism, Critical Utopian Socialism, etc.) Marx himself noted in the *Communist Manifesto* –forms in which it keeps reappearing from time to time. In other words, socialism came up long before Soviet Union did, and we are socialist because of capitalism and not because of Soviet Union. Some of us were in fact socialist despite Soviet Union. And socialism remains on the agenda of history so long as capitalism lasts.

For Marx, socialism is essentially a negation of capitalism, a negation of its economy, politics and ethical-aesthetic values, its multiple alienations and commodification of life. There are no blueprints of socialist society of the future in Marx's social theory. His scientific method forbidding any such speculation, Marx simply refused to 'compose the music of the future'. As 'the most radical rupture' in human history, he visualised the construction of socialism, or communist society proper, as constituting a long period of transition. But the problems of this transition were never seriously discussed or theorised by Marx.

There are only scattered references to it in different writings of Marx and Engels, concerned primarily with characteristics of socialism as a transitional society between capitalism and communism (which they regarded as the goal towards which history was moving). The most important single document of classical Marxism here, that is, on the subject of construction of a new socialist society, is Marx's *Critique of the Gotha Programme* – really Marx's marginal notes to the programme of the German Workers Party, published by Engels after Marx's death, sixteen years after Marx wrote them. The very title is significant. The only time Marx is drawn into making somewhat detailed, yet all too brief, comment on the subject, it is as a critique of his own party or followrs in Germany for their confused and shoddy thinking over several issues, which also included that concerning the socialist society of the future – a critique distinguished for 'the ruthless severity' and 'mercilessness' typical of Marx in matters of theory. To be specifically noted here is that Marx never saw socialism, 'advanced', 'developed', or anyother, as a social formation existing in its own right (as Soviet Marxism did); that would be plainly violative of its essential character as Marx defined it, that is a transition between capitalism and communism. As was common in his times, there is a certain loose usage of the term 'socialism' in Karl Marx. Quite often he used 'socialism' and 'communism' as synonymous terms, both referring to the same kind of society, that is, a 'cooperative society' or 'association' based on 'free associated labour'. More specifically, it is what Marx called 'the first phase of communist society' which later Marxists, including Lenin, came to describe as 'socialism' (as opposed to 'communism' proper). Marx therefore, nowhere speaks of 'socialism' as a distinct stage or social formation or of 'transition between socialism and communism'. For Marx, as the new society emerges from the capitalist society itself, the former is obviously an integral part of the same new society, being its 'first phase' only chronologically, with the specific kind of developments corresponding to it. For him, between capitalism and communism lies no stage or stages, only a transition, more or less prolonged according to circumstances, possibly a whole epoch or perhaps even more than one historical epoch. Lenin, though sharing the loose usage often equated socialism with communism, was equally explicit in speaking of 'transition period between capitalism and communism'...

I would suggest that Marx's view here is theoretically correct and politically more fruitful as against positing the transition in terms of stages such as 'new democracy', 'people's democracy', 'revolutionary democracy', 'socialist society', etc.

That there is no fore-ordained model or blueprint of socialism or socialist transition, certainly none suitable for all countries and all times, does not mean absence of general principles that flow from the Marxist tradition, the experience gained in national liberation and social revolutionary struggles and the efforts at socialist construction so far. For this reason critical understanding of Marxist tradition and revolutionary struggles of the past, and an equally critical analysis of and drawing of lessons from the past experiments in socialism, even when they have failed, is more than an intellectual game; it is an urgent and practical necessity for socialists everywhere, including those in the third world, seeking a proper perpective on possible socialist transition in their countries.

Again, socialism, for Marx, is not just a set of humane economic arrangements, it is an emancipatory project. Marx saw socialism in its transition to communism as humankind's transition to 'the realm of freedom' which according to him lies beyond material pursuits, beyond all activity geared to economic needs. He wrote:

> ... The realm of freedom actually begins only where labour which is determined by necessity and mundane consideration ceases; thus in the very nature of things it lies beyond the sphere of actual material production. Just as the savage must wrestle with nature to satisfy his wants, to maintain and reproduce life, so must civilised man, and he must do so in all social formations and under all modes of production... Freedom in this field can only consist in socialised man, the associated producers, rationally regulating their interchange with nature, bringing it under their common control, instead of being ruled by it as by a blind power, and achieving this with the least expenditure of energy and under conditions most favourable to and worthy of, their human nature. But it nonetheless still remain a realm of necessity. Beyond it begins that development of human power which is an end in itself, the true realm of freedom, which, however, can blossom forth only with this realm of necessity as its basis.

The aspiration or vision that Marx here sets forth is in fact as old as civilisation; it is there, for instance, in Plato and Aristotle, though its realisation, then and afterwards, was seen possible only for a few. Marx put more substance into this aspiration and sought its realisation for *all* human beings. In other words, economic activity was throughout deemed to have meaning only if it serves something other than itself. For Marx this is activities 'valued as an end in themselves'(as he phrased it in the *Grundrisse*), which for him is indeed 'the true measure of wealth'.

Marx, in line with his mode of thinking, took a historical

view of the growth of needs and desires of human beings as one aspect of the general development of human nature, which is also the subjective aspect of the growth of human powers and capacities. His argument is suggestive of an infinite future of creation and cultivation of 'the wealth of subjective *human* sensitivity', of specifically human senses, which is really the same as human nature all the time *becoming more human*. And the important point is that, for Marx, the exercise of these naturally and historically produced specifically human senses – the sense for music and poetry, art, science and history, love, justice and compassion, and so on – constituted the very essence of a truly human appropriation of life and nature, a genuinely rich human life. That is how in pointing out the alienating, depersonalising and dehumanising consequences of capitalism, Marx particularly focused attention on the fact that for all these glorious human senses, whose active and concrete exercise alone constitutes the true content of a genuinely rich human life, capitalism substitutes a single abstract sense, the sense for property, a particular, historically transient, substitute sense which plays havoc with human personality and plunges man, in the words of Ladislav Stoll, 'into the terrible inner sickness of a dehumanised world'. Marx wrote: 'In place of *all* these physical and mental senses there has ...come the sheer estrangement of *all* these senses – the sense of *having*. The human being had to be reduced to this absolute poverty in order that he might yield his inner wealth to the outer world'. 'The more you *have*', said Marx, 'the less you *are*'. Hence his insistence that 'the transcendence of private property is therefore the complete *emancipation* of all human senses and attributes'. He spoke of communism, 'the *actual* phase necessary for the next stage of historical development in the process of human emancipation and recovery', 'as the positive transcendence of *private property as human self-estrangement*, and therefore as the real *appropriation of the human essence* by and for man; communism therefore as the complete return of man to himself as a *social* (i.e., human) being – a return become conscious, and accomplished within the entire wealth of previous development.' Marx added: 'What is to be evoided above all is the re-establishing of "society" as an abstraction *vis-a-vis* the individual. The individual *is the social being*. His life... is therefore an expression and confirmation of *social life*.' Marx is an individualist in the basic sense that his ultimate vision was a society where every individual could be a fully human being, where, as Marx himself put it, 'the free development of each is the condition for the free development of all'...

Such is the fulfilment Marx's socialism/communism seeks for humankind. As Engels expressed it, 'it is humanity's leap from the realm of necessity into the realm of freedom', the end of its 'pre-history' and the beginning of 'truly human history'.

Yet again, socialism, for Marx, is nothing inevitable, it is something to be struggled for.

Marx was no determinist, ever. Whatever determinism there is in his Marxism, is a most conditional one, which accords primacy to human praxis, to revolutionary politics. If attention was drawn to the economic-structural necessities underlying the historical processes, it was for enhancing the freedom for praxis, for not foreclosing but liberating human practice, for freer choices by humans, free not in some abstract or metaphysical sense, but in the only possible human sense of men and women choosing and acting with the fullest possible knowledge and consideration of the necessities of the objective material situation or circumstances. Such is the dialectics of freedom and necessity in Marx.

Thus there are no inevitabilities in Marx and no guarantees of victory either, only alternatives. Even as he insisted in the *Communist Manifesto* that 'the history of all hitherto existing society is the history of class struggle'. Marx had immediately added that this struggle 'each time ended, either in a revolutionary reconstitution of society at large, or in the common ruin of the contending classes'. Again, he had hailed the productive achievements of capitalism – 'it has been the first to show what man's activity can bring about', creating 'more massive and more colossal productive forces than have all preceding generations together' (*Communist Manifesto*). But he had also pointed out not only the damage that capitalism regularly inflicts upon humans and nature but also its long term destructive potential – 'its accumulation process', Marx wrote in *Grundrisse*, can have 'the consequences even for the total destruction of humanity' – a prognosis which Rosa Luxemburg later summed up as the alternative: 'socialism or barbarism'.

Incidentally, these alternatives to socialism – the threat of 'common ruin of the contending classes', and 'the total destruction of humanity' are already a part of the reality of our world today.

For whatever reasons, which certainly included an underestimation of capitalism's productive potential and resilience, Marx gave capitalism a short lease of life, which allowed for the possibility of realising socialism as an emancipatory project, that is initiating the epochal transition this project implied. In his main theory on the subject, based on his view of the historical tendencies of advanced capitalist development in Europe, Marx visualised the necessity as well as the possibilityof a transition from capitalism to socialism/communism in the countries of advanced industrial development, with their mature productive basis and proletarian presence – 'Empirically, communism is only possible as the act of the dominant peoples "all at once" and simultaneously, which presupposes the universal development of productive forces and the world intercourse bound up with them', is how Marx put it in *The German Ideology*. Accordingly, Marx looked forward to an early revolution in Europe – though he also recognized (in a letter to Engels in 1858): 'For us the difficult question is this: the revolution on the Continent is imminent and its character will be at once socialist; will it not be necessarily crushed in this little corner of the world, since on a much larger terrain the development of bourgeois society is still in the ascendant'. The hoped-for European revolution finally arrived in the aftermath of the first world war but it survied only in Russia, confronting Lenin and his Bolsheviks with a totally unanticipated task: attempt a socialist transition in a single backward country, a situation or possibility that was never theorized by Marx. And now, though not inevitable, the attempt has failed. History seems to have played a trick on the doctrine of Karl Marx. This trick including the failure in the Soviet Union is eminently amenable to explanation in terms of this very doctrine but more important is to note the consequent reality of the contemporary world in relation to Marx's own perspective on transition to socialism and the struggle for socialism in our times.

Of this reality three features need to be particularly noticed.

The most important, of course, is that , as a capitalist world, it is a world of 'overdeveloped', 'underdeveloped' or so-called 'developing' countries. The latter two categories are generally well understood but we need to take a closer look at the 'overdeveloped' countries of advanced capitalism. For one, capitalism survives and is indeed dominant today, but, as noticed earlier, it remains a failed system.

Again, that capitalism continues to survive, by itself cannot be seen as an argument for the desirability, or a sign of the progressiveness, of the capitalist order, much less as any sort of 'trimph' of capitalism. 'That position', says Paul Baran, 'is no more defensible than would be the view that an inability of the human body to resist tuberculosis, however caused, furnishes a proof of the harmlessness or even usefulness of that illness'.

He adds 'The failure of an irrationally organised society to generate internal forces pressing towards and resulting in its abolition and replacement by a more rational, more human social relations results necessarily in economic stagnaion, cultural decay, and a widespread sense of despondency. Such a society – even if once the most advanced in the world – loses its position of leadership, slides into the backwaters of historical development and turns into a breeding ground of reaction, inhumanity and obscurantism.' With the damage done by the continued extence of capitalism, this is indeed the case today, not only in the United States but increasingly in the other so-called advanced societies of late capitalism.

U.S. leading, these societies are, in a profound sense, to a greater or lesser degree, sick societies. Concerned scholars have written of the phenomenon of 'alienation' in these societies, their citizens' growing sense of anomie and estrangement, of isolation, hostility and frustration. They are sick with these and hundred other social and psychic ailments born of prolonged living under an essentially irrational system, sick with apathy and boredom, with 'other-directedness' and conformism, with fears, insecurities and neuroses of all kinds. Their sustained social regression is reflected as much in the reaction and obscurantism they breed, their frivolous consumption and culture of drugs, and even guns, as in the debilitating barrage of fraudulent politics, barren culture and stupefying entertainment, inspirational rackets and demoralising press, and comic books, to which their people, even otherwise ill-educated, are exposed all the time. Societies in the grip of crises which they cannot resolve, they are inevitably producing deep pathological deformations which manifest themselves variously in different places as racism, sexism, anti-Semitism, xenophobia, ethnic or national hatreds, fundamentalism and intolerance, even as plain cruelty and aggression. Poverty, unemployment and insecurity-related crimes and associated phenomena – ill health and suicides, alcoholism and drug addiction, racist discrimination and criminal violence, violence against women and child abuse, etc. – are on the rise everywhere. In many of these 'advanced' societies marginal indigenous populations are rapidly being wiped out for one reason or another. By their very nature profoundly immoral societies, based as they are on domination and exploitation of man by man, along with humanistic values and culture and all human relationships, even their professed moralities and principles now stand devastated by the morality and values of 'the market'. And, most significantly, there is the near-absence of ideals in these societies, of any concern for a better future to strive for, that has been the motive force of all human progress in the past. The instruments of communication and discovery invented by their technological genius have become the means of debasing people's understanding and preventing them from looking beyond the capitalist horizon.

I may here quote a passage from *Crisis of Socialism—Notes in Defence of a Mommitment* which is in its own way relevant to the point being made:

> In the midst of capitalist triumphalism following the collapse of the Soviet Union, David Harvey had written: '...we live in an age of political celebration of the virtues of entrepreneurial capitalism and individualism, in an era when our technological confidence appears unbounded... and when spatial barriers are crumbling. Yet it is also an era... (which) reflects a crisis of capitalism of the deepest magnitude – a crisis that flexible accumulation has not resolved given its paltry rates of growth, the painful devaluations, the increasing class polarisations, the increasing political tensions – all in the midst of extraordinary instability, insecurity, fragmentation and change'. The crisis has only deepened since then and the new century has opened in the midst of an all-pervasive economic, moral, cultural and intellectual disarray and a consumerist deterioration of individual and social life. The collapse of socialism has made the unacceptable consequences of capitalism all the more visible and vicious, and exposed the inadequacy of different variants of social democracy as well as the irrelevance of the dominant theories of growth and development, their 'assorted medications' for economic and social ills that are now chronic at home and abroad. There is widespread political and social instability, economic chaos, corruption at the highest levels of society and above all 'a shrivelling of the spirit'

> as it has been described. Science, reason, progress, the entire inheritance of the age of Enlightenment and the great revolutions is being questioned and abandoned, the predominance of morally destructive consumerism is accompanied by a fashionable post-modernism's nihilistic relativism concerning matters of truth, knowledge, or morals. And the world over there is the rising incidence of xenophobic nationalism, racism, religiosity and fundamentalist revivalism, religious and ethnic strife, tribal and national conflicts, and the exhibition of raw power in both private and public spheres. There is pervasive lament over the sorry shape of things in the world, east or west. A sign of times, scholars have turned to Toynbee and his discourse on the disintegration of civilisations whose cause, according to him, lies in 'schism of the soul', in the 'personal crises of behaviour and feeling and life which are the true essence and origin of the visible manifestations of social collapse.' They have been discussing both the causes and symptoms of disintegration in the countries of Western Europe and its offshoot on the other side of the Atlantic, the United States, Decades ago Lewis Mumford had writtten of 'a blankness, a sterility, a boredom, a despair' that had, at deeper levels come to characterise modern, that is capitalist society. Today all this has surfaced with a vengeance in the alienated sociaties of capitalism. We have the lament of Leszek Kolakowski: 'Whatever area of life we reflect upon, the natural instinct is to ask: what is wrong with it? And indeed we keep asking: What's wrong with God? With democracy? With Socialism? With art? With sex? With the family? With economic growth?... it seems as though we live with the feeling of an all-encompassing crisis without being able, however, to identify its causes.' Gramsci had once written, of course of a different historical juncture: 'The old is dying and the new cannot be born; in this interregnum a great variety of morbid symptoms appear'. These 'morbid symptoms' are, to a greater or lesser degree, there all over the advanced and less advanced capitalist countries today, as good an evidence as any of the deep crisis of the capitalist civilisation, of the ultimate failure of capitalism in our times.

Indeed, the sickness of these so-called advanced societies, the spiritual disarray of the capitalist civilisation they represent, is nowhere more evident than in their cynical idealisation of capitalism as it exists and utter lack of any vision of a secure and more satisfying life beyond their 'consumerist heaven of instant gratification', a life which would be satisfactory of basic human needs – decent livelihood, knowledge, solidarity, cooperation with fellow human beings, gratification in work and freedom from toil – and provide the possibility of men and women appropriating the world with all their glorious human senses. It needs to be added that these societies are all the more sick societies because they need to change the existing state of affairs but are unable to generate the necessary social forces for carrying out the revolutionary change they so badly need.

The continuance of capitalism as 'sick' societies of advanced capitalist west has an important implicaton. In a sense socialism arrived a little before its time, attempted as it was first in Russia, a society that was not prepared to build it. The Bolsheviks had to contend with the problems of a backward, underdeveloped capitalist-feudal social order, problems which caused grave distortions and contributed to the ultimate failure of their attempted transition to socialism. Those who may be called upon to build a late-arrived socialism in advanced capitalist countries will have to contend with equally difficult but *different* problems of an 'overdeveloped' capitalism – a capitalism living beyond its time as it were, beyond the period of 'its historical legitimacy' In other words, as with 'underdevelopment', 'overdevelopment', too poses its own unanticipated problems for the realisation of Marx's project of socialism.

Socialism, of course, remains on the agenda wherever capitalism exists, be it 'overdeveloped', 'underdevelped', 'developing' or any other. And there is always the overarching question as to what kind of society we, as *human beings*, want to have. Surely it is people and not 'economic growth' or productivity that must come first in such a society. It has to be a humane society that fosters cooperation, solidarity and respect for universal ethical values, and makes for a non-alienated, 'truly rich human life' that Marx spoke of. Of course such a society is impossible without basic material security and need satisfaction. But to believe that you can assure need satisfaction through greed, private acquisitive drives, universal competition and strife – the values of capitalism – and yet hope for a humane society of cooperation and solidarity is utopianism of the worst kind. Subordinating humanity to economics, to imperatives of the market, capitalism commodifies life and undermines and rots away the relations betwen human beings which constitute societies. Its ethos of the marketplace – competition, egoism, aggression, alienation, universal venality, in short the rat race – creates a moral vacuum in which nothing counts except what the individual wants and can grab, here and now. At the end of it all, even when wants are satisfied, the people are ever more subordinated, ever less free, ever more flattened and made passive by the dictatorship of consumerism, that arbitrarily shapes values, imposing on them the heavy burden of uniformity. The values of difference, individualisation (not individualism), all-sided development of man, of human freedom itself disappear in the market place which is proclaimed to be free. As human beings, people simply don't fit into capitalism, which is a quintessential market society. For a truly humane society to come into existence, capitalism has to go.

But, in view of their 'overdevelped', 'underdeveloped' or 'developing' character, to speak of socialism in relation to these capitalist societies is not to posit socialism as achievable today or tomorrow, or even the day after, but, as suggested earlier, to posit it as people's alternative strategic goal, as the principle governing people's politics which links together their immediate ongoing and emerging struggles in an ultimate project of revolutionary transformation of society, as the goal of a long transitional process whose specifics and speed will depend on the objective material conditions and the nature and balance of class forces involved at each stage of the struggle.

In other words, while expressions like 'building socialism'

or 'building socialism of the 21st century' have a certain historical and political legitimacy, what is on the agenda is a socialism-oriented development, such that, no matter how slow or halting or contradictions-laden, it is a development *away from* capitalism and the imperatives of its market and *towards* Marx's emancipatory vision of socialism, which was, in any case, visualised as a transition spanning an entire epoch, even more than one epoch.

This, again, is not to suggest any 'model of socialist politics'. Just as there is no single or foreordained model of socialism, one that is suitable for all climes and all times, there is none of socialist politics either. The specific conditions or demands and the forms of struggle they generate will vary from country to country. Which however, does not mean the absence of general principles to guide it that flow from the Marxist tradition and the experiance gained in social revolutionary and national liberation struggles. The recovery of these principles is in fact a must for any successful pursuit of socialist politics today.

The two other features of the changed reality of the world in relation to Marx's perspective and the struggle for socialism today, each important in its own way, may also be noted. Firstly, since global capitalism is nationally organised and immediately dependent on national states, national economies and national states remain the primary terrain of anti-capitalist organisation and struggle. Of course, an international perspective, working people's solidarity across national frontiers, remains vital to any socialist movement. And today there exists a focus for such solidarity as has, perhaps, never before existed in the history of capitalism. The universalisation of capitalism has not brought about the cessation but instead the universalisation of struggle against capitalism. When, with globalisation, just about every state is following the same destructive logic, domestic struggles against that common logic can be the basis – in fact the strongest possible basis – of a new internationalism. But looking for that internationalism must not be an excuse for giving up on local, national struggles. The main arenas of struggle against global capitalism still remain local and national. 'Workers of all countries, unite' remains the motto but this 'unity' obviously begins at home. There is a growing space for common transnational struggles, but the established order has still to be primality fought on our own home pitch. As the *Manifesto* put it a long time ago: 'the proletariat of each country must, of course, first of all settle matters with its own bourgeoisie.' If the historical experience of more than a century since the Paris Commune is any guide, this is exactly how it has been, the world revolutionary process has turned out to be extremely uneven and has moved from country to country.

In other words, the nation state is indeed the concrete terrain on which the struggle for the radical transformation of society must begin and may have to be carried forward. It may be added that to argue that a nationa state – and this includes states of the size and resources of Britain, France or Italy, or for that matter, India, China or Russia – cannot provide the ground on which the radical transformation of society can be attemped is to rule out such a transition for the forthcoming historical period. It is to abdicate the struggle for socialism in our time.

Secondly, it was Marx's prognosis that capitalism in its ultimate consequences could spell even 'the total destruction of humanity'. But giving capitalism a short lease of life, Marx never explored this distant possibility. The distant possibility is now an imminent threat hanging over the future of humankind. As noted earlier, Rosa Luxemburg had summed up Marx's prognosis in her famous poser: 'socialism or barbarism'. Capitalism living beyond its historical time indeed spells a future of barbarism for humankind. It could be a nuclear holocaust that its politics has threatened for more than half a century or the almost certain ecological disaster which – noise over so-called 'sustainable development' notwithstanding – capitalism's accumulative logic now portends. This makes the struggle for socialism all the more imperative and urgent today.

•

No argument for socialism today can bypass what happened in the erstwhile Soviet Union. What we have here, as I have argued at length in my *Crisis of Socialism – Notes in Defence of a Commitment,* is a failed revolutionary experiement: a grievously deformed socialism that was built and the final crisis and collapse of the *sui generis* class exploitative system it had ultimately degenerated into – all of which is fully amenable to a Marxist explanation in terms of its method of historical materialism and class analysis. In other word, what failed in Soviet Union was not socialism but a system that came to be built in its name. I have no time to discuss this subject here. I will later only take note of a major deformation of Soviet socialism which the socialist project today needs to dissociate from. Immediately I would only like to emphasise the need for socialists and communists to understand the why and how, and the implications, of what happened in the erstwhile Soviet Union.

It is indeed imperative for socialists/communists who wish for a future beyond capitalism, to understand what has happened, what was built and what has failed as socialism in the Soviet Union. They must assess the costs and consequences of this failure, the collapse of what we have described as 'actually existing socialism', and some others as 'authoritarian communism' – though they must do so fully mindful of the costs and consequences of 'actually existing capitalism' or 'authoritarian capitalism' which has rushed in to pick up the pieces. It was certainly mistaken to see the struggle for socialism in our times as a contest betwen 'the socialist world' and 'the capitalist world', as official Marxism in the post- 1917 period made it out to be. It was, as always, an international class struggle with several more or less important fronts. The countries of 'actually existing socialism', while it lasted, were only one front of this struggle, and while they did condition or influence this struggle, positively as well as negatively, they did not determine or settle the question of its outcome. Nor does the collapse of these countries now, or their return to the capitalist fold, in any way settle the question of the future of socialism – the struggle still goes on and will, so long as capitalism lasts. Nevertheless, these countries constituted what was in many ways a most important front of the on-going international class struggle and their collapse demands that socialists and communists understand and come to terms with it. If they no more need to carry the burden of a deformed and degenerated socialism or be answerable for its ugliness and cruelties, the burden of a genuine, Marxist explanation of its collapse has still to be carried by them so that our people know the truth and appropriate lessons are drawn for struggles of the future.

We need this explanation not only to learn the right and not wrong lessons from what has happened, but even more because in the absence of *our* explanation, it is *their*, the enemies' explanation which will continue to prevail, and this is: 'socialism has failed'. What is more, we need it to prevent *them* from taking our history away from us. For the ideologues of capitalism, even as they have pronounced the 'end of socialism' and with the post-modernists even deny the ability to learn from history, are busy depicting the October and what followed, an entire era of people's heroic struggles and achievements, as nothing but a costly aberration in history. Indeed, defending or reclaiming our history is today in itself a revolutionary project for us, as part of our assessment of what has happened in the Soviet Union.

The lessons, often bitter ones, have to be drawn from the past. This is necessary to face reality and rebuild the required politics and culture on the Left. But it is equally necessary to be properly balanced about it. In other words, it also needs to be recognised that this past is not entirely a bitter heritage. Our assessment or self-accounting must not throw any baby out with the bath water.

An assessment or reassessment of the experience of Soviet Union, culminating in the collapse of history's first great experiment in socialism and of the whole communist movement associated with it, even when not led or dominated by it, is obviously important for socialists and communists everywhere, in the North as well as the South. But those who especially need to master the lessons of this experience are the leaders and even more the militant cadre of the communist parties for whom Soviet Union was a decisive point of reference and identity, whatever the differences that may have emerged in the later period. In the West, unable or unwilling to find answers to the Soviet collapse and related problems from within Marxism, most of these parties have simply abandoned the socialist project and opted for the social democratic road. Elsewhere, mostly in the third world, though remaining formally communist, they are confused and disoriented by what has happened, and unable to transcend the orthodoxies of 'official Marxism' are content to blame it all on Khrushchevite revisionism, betrayal of a Gorbachev or secret machinations of U.S. imperialism and its CIA. Even the Marxist-Leninist communist formations, or those holding on to the old orthodoxies of Chinese vintage, have, by and large, failed to go beyond this much too simplistic and shallow understanding. Unless the opportunity is now seized to turn to authentic, creative Marxism to understand the crisis and collapse of Soviet socialism and this understanding made central to a rethinking of the whole question of the long current reformist or ultra-left practices in the movement, the momentum of the past may keep these communist parties going, but with the old leaders and credibility born of past struggles or gains fading out and the failure of any new radical recruitment, they can only stagnate, or continue to decline down the road of economistic practices, electoralist reforms and even pragmatic adjustments within the ongoing capitalist globalisation; as to the Marxist-Leninist or Maoist formations their avowed revolutionary commitment notwithstanding, they will remain the sectarian movements they are, wrangling with each other and quarantined within their limited areas of influence. Though communist in name, these parties and formations will have lost the opportunity to recover and become a politically effective force on behalf of socialism.

For socialists in the third world, including those who call themselves communists, the Soviet experience has an added, rather exceptional importance. Classical Marxism, with its perspective of construction of socialism in advanced capitalist countries and on an international scale, had, apart from some general principle, little to say to the Russian Bolsheviks as they set out on their unanticipated journey in an entirely uncharted territory, a struggle for socialism in a single backward country, in the midst of unremitting hostility of internationally dominant capitalism led by its most advanced sectors. Theirs was a pioneering effort. Insofar as the cause of its failure lies, along with the force of objective circumstances, in the inadequacies of theory and practice for this unprecedented task, the Soviet experience has invaluable lessons for revolutionaries in the third world as, like Russia, their poor and backward countries, in this period of renewed global capitalist domination, seek a better, necessarily socialist, destiny for themselves.

What has happened in the former Soviet Union does not in any way invalidate Marx's argument for the necessity and possibility of a socialist negation of capitalist social order. Only the struggle for socialism is turning out to be far more complex and difficult than he ever visualised. Socialists or Communists, of course, have no illusions that the struggle for socialism is going to be easy or expeditiously successful. After the first failure it will be far more difficult in many ways than before, it is going to be a long detour to socialism next time. But they have no reason to feel gloomy about the prospects either. The material conditions are more favourable and objective compulsions far stronger than appeared possible a few years ago, and the constituency for the socialist cause can only grow as capitalism shows itself increasingly incapable of coping with the crises it produces.

•

As suggested above, the advocacy of socialism-oriented development or citing of Soviet achievement in support, needs to be dissociated from the authoritarianism that Soviet experiment in socialism was associated with.

It can be legitimately argued that the failure of this experiment occurred essentially on the political terrain, as a consequences of the politics practised over a very long period. Insofar as it is politics that commands economy under socialism, even the economic failure, whatever its autonomous causation, cannot be dissociated from the politics that ultimately governed it. Therefore, it is here, in the realm of politics, that the more basic lessons of Soviet experience lie. More specifically, the most decisive of these lessons concerns the issue of democracy in a socialist transition. Whatever their economic and social achievements or failures, the greatest failure of the societies of 'actually existing socialism' was in the area of building socialist democracy, a self-governing society of the associated producers and reproducers that socialism postulates. Instead, though born of socialist revolutions, they became each a grossly undemocratic system whose authoritarian politics bred extraordinary corruption of power at the top and became a decisive factor in the ultimate collapse of the system itself. If, issues of theory apart, we were looking for the *single most important right lesson* to be drawn from the Soviet experience, it can be legitimately located in relation to democracy, which 'Soviet socialism' signally failed to practice, even though it is visualised by classical Marxism to be integral to a socialist transition anywhere. It is indeed so integral to socialism as a value and as a necessity that one can say, socialism will be democratic or it will not *be*.

As Marxists, the Bolsheviks were indeed committed to democracy as they set out on the road to socialism. Democracy was the pervasive feature of Soviet life and activity in the immediate aftermath of the Octorber Revolution. As Neil Harding has put it:

> The objective of the socialist revolution was, as Lenin once pithily put it, 'an end of bossing' and this, in a nutshell, was the message of *State and Revolution*. Its challenge was the promethean one, born of the impeccable line of Marx's romantic view of man as actor, the forger of his own world. It ran directly counter to that other Saint Simonian development of social democratic Marxism which saw the individual as the beneficiary of an efficient state-directed philanthropy. To the war-weary, to the hungry, to the indentured workforce and the oppressed peasantry, Lenin projected in 1917 a vision, a challenge...– power is yours, take it and use it; the land is yours, take and use it, the factories are yours, take them and use them – get off your knees and be men, rule yourselves. This was the message... encapsulated in his slogan 'All Power to the Soviets'. It was an extraordinary platform which called not for the capture of political power by a political party but for the dissolution of the state in an infinitely varied system of soviets and communes.

Such was Lenin's project. It was indeed launched in the period immediately following the October Revolution. But it lasted barely six months. What actually happened over the next few years was something quite different. The immediate exigencies of the infant Soviet state struggling for survival in its isolation took precedence over everything else. Battered by the white armies of foreign intervention, civil war and counter-revolution, ruined industrially and facing economic chaos, threatened with hunger and starvation by famine at home and imperialist blockade from abroad, and all the time confronting the inexorable logic of Russian backwardness, the new Soviet state desperately struggled to stay alive. The social and political pressure, internal and external, was enormous and almost intolerable. And the Bolsheviks' own resources to cope with it were fast getting depleted, seriously blunting the edge of any effective *socialist* political intervention in the situation. Lenin's project, with all its early promise, though never abandoned in theory, simply floundered.

Part of the tragedy of Lenin was that, as within Russia and without, not his hopeful predictions but worst fears came to materialise, as civil war, famine and economic collapse consumed the country and the Bolshevik dream, no matter how valiantly he struggled, Lenin was himself increasingly compelled to retreat, and to compromise. And he did not live long enough to recover and regain the initiative. The assassin's bullets, first incapacitated and finally claimed him in January 1924. Nevertheless, his project and his struggle retain their importance, as Lenin hoped, for 'other revolutions' of the future.

As democracy withered and perished, over time, Soviet Union degenerated into a dictatorial regime to become a most important *negative* factor that has to be now dissociated from the *positive* achievements of Soviet Union as the exemplar of a non-capitalist, socialism-oriented path of development. The regime was claimed to be the 'dictatorship of the proletariat' that Marx had spoken of, which was a gross missrepresentation and mispractice of Marx's famous formulation on the subject. As we have already noticed, Marx simply refused to speculate about the economic or political organisation of the socialist/communist society of the future. If there is little in Marx /Engels about its economic structure beyond some very general propositions, there is even less about its political arrangements. Marx indeed stipulated *a political form* (the proletarian state) under which the transition from the old to the new society was to be accomplished. Viewing capitalism and communism as two distinct societies, each existing in its own right, Marx saw the emerging socialist polity as a transitional period between capitalism and communism in which classes would necessarily persist for a long time, classlessness being a feature not of socialism but of the higher phase of communism. Therefore this period will be characterised by contradictions and conflicts, by class struggle in diverse spheres as its motive force right upto the achievement of a classless and stateless society. In Marx's social theory, any government in a class society, regardless of its specific form – be it democratic or any other – is essentially a dictatorship of the ruling class over the ruled classes. And this is how he visualised the 'dictatorial' state during this transitional period. For Marx, it was to be a regime which, while dictatorial towards the old exploiting classes would be the broadest kind of democracy for the workers and the people in general, much more democratic than the most liberal of bourgeois democracies, extending to the working people all those civil rights and political freedoms through whose exercise alone they could transform themselves into new human beings capable of building a new society. It is in this specific context that he spoke of the 'dictatorship of the proletariat.' Obviously 'dictatorship' here is not something opposed to democracy as the conventional view has it. Marx was only pointing to the essential *social content,* the class character of public or political power in a transitional socialist society—just as, for Marx, even the most democratically organised bourgeois state, in this sense, is yet a 'dictatorship of the bourgeoisie'. In other words, Marx's was not a statement about form of government, its institutional structure or organisation, its parties or politics, or for that matter, any specific 'dictatorial' policies to be pursued. It may be added that Paris Commune, whose democratic organisation and functioning remains unrivalled to this day, was recognised by Marx as an example of the *rule* (or 'dictatorship') of the proletariat. He noticed and underlined the extraordinary advance in democracy which Commune represented both as a form of government and in the measures it carried out. Marx not only saw the extraordinarily democratic Paris Commune as the model of 'the dictatorship of the proletariat', a 'thoroughly expansive' political form for a socialist transition, but, insofar as class struggle continues throughout the transitional period, Marx also viewed it as affording 'the rational medium in which that class struggle can run through its different phases in the most rational and humane way'.

Obviously, Marx's 'dictatorship of the proletariat' never happened in the Soviet Union. It is indeed 'the great absence' in the historical experiment of 'building socialism' in the Soviet Union, (which was at the same time a decisively important factor in its ultimate failure.) Soviet socialism's authoritarian deformation has had the consequence of opening up a gulf between socialism and democracy which was not there earlier. It indeed gifted away democracy to capitalism.

The issue here is important enough to merit a more specific reiteration: Throughout its history socialism and democracy were invariably seen to be positively interlinked. Today the link is tenuous, almost no more, in large part because of the Soviet experience. This experience – its lack of political freedoms and gross abuse of power, its Terror and Gulag and lawless destruction of millions of lives (including those of communists), its offical 'truth' and offical lies, and the travesty of every democratic notion – has left the democratic credentials of socialism badly damaged. In the popular perception, socialism and democracy have become dissociated. Even for well-meaning people socialism has come to be linked with the ideas of a strong, not to say all-powerful, state and with centralised regulation of all aspects of social life. The undemocratic nature of 'Soviet socialism' has enabled the opponents of socialism, in a hegemonic offensive, not only to argue, ever more effectively, that socialism is inherently authoritarian and oppresive but also to counterpose democracy to socialism and appropriate it for capitalism, even restore capitalism in the name or under cover of democracy. It is significant that the upheavals in

Eastern Europe and Soviet Union were guided not by a futuristic vision or by ideals of the past summed up as 'democracy'. 'It was 1789 taking revenge on 1917 in 1989', as one commentator has put it. The 'normal' society sought by those who carried out or supported these upheavals may have meant prosperity of 'free market' and liberal democracy, but in effect democracy came to be identified with the 'free market' so that the 'new democracies' of Eastern Europe, for example, were 'democratic' in proportion to their progress in 'marketisation'. Given this identification, it has become possible to so bypass the issue of capitalism that the question of seeking an alternative to it, of its transcendence in socialism, simply does not arise. In a clever, confusing use of terms, ideologues of capitalism, in the media and the academy, on occasion helped even by some 'progressive' critics of the Soviet system, present the issue as democracy versus socialism. Thus instead of socialism being an alternative to capitalism, democracy itself is frequently put forward as an alternative to socialism – a view that has been superficially strengthened by the return of 'multiparty democratic politics' to Russia and Eastern Europe in conjunction with the drive towards full restoration of capitalism. The ideologues proclaim that in opposing 'communism', they are defending democracy against its enemies on the left, whether those enemies called themselves Communists, Socialists, or whatever. The Western campaign in support of democracy becomes an attack on socialism. Perhaps the greatest of all successes which capitalist ideologues and politicians have scored in their struggle for hegemony has been in the appropriation of democracy as their particular cause and concem.

Hence the need to dissociate socialism from its authoritarian deformation, to recover democracy for socialism. Incidentally, it is authoritarianism associated with socialism (largely because of Soviet experience) which allows a free marketing Obama to dismiss the socialist choice of a democratically planned economy, that is democracy in the sphere of economy, as 'an oppressive government-run economy' and which is an important reason why, as more than one bourgios ideologue has noted with obvious relief, the current crisis of capitalism has not produced a corresponding advocacy of socialism. This makes it all the more necessary to recover democracy for socialism.

•

Recovering democracy for socialism raises a host of issues for socialist politics, among them the most important issue of pursuit of revolutionary politics in regimes of bourgeois democracy, apropos which Ralph Miliband, with the bitter Soviet experience in mind, has written:

> Regimes which do, either by necessity or choice, depend on the suppression of all opposition and the stifling of all civic freedoms must be taken to represent a disastrous regression, in political terms, from bourgeois democracy whatever the economic and social achievements of which they must be capable... The civic freedoms which, however inadequately, form part of bourgeois democracy are the product of centuries of unremitting popular struggles. The task of Marxist politics is to defend these freedoms and to make possible their enlargement by the removal of their class boundaries.

The issue here is one of topical importance and I would like to share an argument over it:

Revolution is not only armed struggle or insurrection, though these still cannot be ruled out. It does not all all help to see revolution as a punctual moment in history or in terms of iconic images like the taking of the Winter Palace or the storming of the Bastille. Revolution is best understood as a comple process of *structural transformation of society* – with special complexities of its own in regimes of bourgeois democracy. In other words, revolutionary politics does not mean thinking and acting in terms of storming the Bastille or seizing the Winter Palace, or launching an immediate armed struggle. There are socialists and communists for whom revolutionary politics is unthinkable except in association with a revolutionary upheaval. For them the task is to set about organising this upheaval, 'to make a revolution'— anything else is dangerous and discredited reformism. This is a wholly mistaken view in that it misses out on the necessarily long period of preparatory ideological and political struggles that go into the making of a socialist revolution, even if it is viewed as an upheaval. At its worst this view even ends up as so much posturing, an alibi for doing nothing. This is not to deny or foreclose the issue that situations may be there in some parts of the world where the main task is to concentrate on organising a revolution, though even here success is most likely only if the task is undertaken with due care and preparation, which does not necessarily rule out all 'reformist' activity. But the situation generally, and certainly in most parts of world today is one of long haul. The main task here is to reach out to the people, organise their class and mass struggles, constantly raise these struggles to the level of political struggles, and relate them to the overall objective of revolutionary transformation of society, the socialist revolution we seek. It is only through such struggles that people will learn to need and make this revolution, whatever eventual shape or form it takes.

This is not an easy task to carry out. Here we are indeed face to face with a problem that is as old as socialism itself. The movement for socialism has an inevitable duality within it. A socialist movement has to fight within the framework of existing capitalist society but must inevitably offer solutions which ultimately lie beyond that framework; it has to struggle for a socialist future from within a capitalist present. If it concentrates too much on that future it runs the risk of sectarian isolation. Yet if it limits itself to struggle within the system, it loses its original *raison d'etre*, the search for a radically different society. The task for the socialist movement thus is to preserve a permanent link between its current partial or defensive struggles and its vision of a future socialist society which is at once distant and crucial. As the *Communist Manifesto* has it:

> The Communists fight for the attainment of the immediate aims, for the enforcement of the momentary interests of the working class; but in the movement of the present, they also represent and take care of the future of that movement.

At the tactical level we have the Leninist insistence that socialists must constantly relate specific grievances to a criticism of the system *as a whole*, constantly showing how they are linked together and therefore how people's specific struggles are also linked to the struggle for a revolutionary transformation of society. In other words, the key task is to establish linkages between theory and practice which would lead everyday resistance beyond short-term demands towards socialism. As Lenin, among many others including Gramsci, understood, these linkages did not spontaneously emerge from ordinary working class life or struggle. It was up to socialists to perceive them theoretically and then forge them into practices or actions which made sense to the working people and linked their orgoing struggles to the coming of a socialist future.

Though easy to formulate in theory, what is involved here is possiby the most difficult yet vital practical task in the struggle for socialism: to link the *immediate* (necessarily reformist) activity with the *ultimate* (essentially revolutionary) objectives; or to phrase it differently, to preserve the integrity of the *ultimate* perspective without losing contact with the *immediate* demands, determinations and potentialities of the historically given condition. Struggle for the immediate or limited aims and objectives is how people, necessarily, begin their struggle against the system and for a better life. Important as a way of saying '*No*' to capitalism in a concrete manner or winning gains for the people, given *socialist* leadership, this struggle can also be a means of enhancing people's consciousness and organisation for the ultimate socialist transformation. Reform and revolution thus must not be seen as mutually exclusive opposites. The task rather is to subordinate reform to revolution.

This is how Marx had argued in his controversy with Bakunin and anarchists. As a revolutionary, Marx rejected voluntarism. As against his opponents who tended to rely on 'spontaneity' and 'instinctive conscience of the popular masses', Marx viewed the development of a *socialist mass consciousness* as necessary for a socialist revolutionary reconstruction of society. For him, this was possible only through struggles over a long period.

Thus, even as we recognise that struggle for socialism, as always, is a *revolutionary* struggle and that socialist politics is nothing if it is not *revolutionary* politics, it does not mean any kind of rejection of reforms. What is demanded is that socialists struggle for reforms as revolutionaries, that is, they remain faithful to socialist principles, imbue the necessarily partial popular struggles with socialist conciousness, put *socialist meaning* into people's experience as they struggle for, win or lose, reforms, and thus help them become more effective subjects or makers of the socialist revolution, in whatever shape or form it has to be eventually made.

This also points to the right perspective for the revolutionary Left's participation in electoral or parliamentary politics. There is no denying that this politics has built-in pressures towards reformism. But this by itself is not and cannot be an argument against participation in such politics, against the use of electoral or parliamentary politics as part of the revolutionary struggle against capitalism. As argued for above, what is important here is the meaning you put into it, the ideology or political consciousness that informs such participation, or for that matter, the struggle against capitalism as a whole. Every form of political activity or struggle is potentially 'reformist' if it is conducted in ideological and organisational isolation from the broader struggle where the capitalist system is the enemy to confront, if the immediate struggle is not linked to the ultimate or strategic object of a socialist transformation of society. Reform, a contest with the ruling class where you are, or within the existing institutions, is where you begin the revolution — and you cannot begin it otherwise, elsewhere. But it is a beginning, a part of revolutionary process only if it is suffused with the revolutionary consiciousness of a socialist. What is really involved here is the relation between reform and revolution where its mistaken understanding has often seen it as an either or question and thus counterposed one against the other. A proper understanding, as Marx, the active revolutionary, himself emphasised, says 'yes' to both but insists that in revolutionary politics reform needs to be subordinated to revolution. A revolutionary struggle against capitalism, therefore, does not in any way rule out the exercise of the rights of bourgeois democracy or the use of its institutions as futile. On the contrary, and very rightly too, revolutionary socialist politics enjoins such exercise and use whenever, wherever and to the degree, possible. And this, in principle, includes participation in electoral or parliamentary politics. To argue for such participation is not to deny or overlook either the ultimately violent nature of the bourgeois democratic state or the subordination of the electoral-parliamentary regimes to the rules established by this state. It is to suggest that notwithstanding its problems and pitfalls, or 'civilising' influence on the revolutionaries, electoral or parliamentary politics can be and needs to be treated as another arena of class struggle, where openings are available for ideological-political struggle against the capitalist social order, where we can carry our own agenda to a vast potential constituency of ours, where we can educate and organise people for non-electoral, extra parliamentary revolutionary socialist politics. What is ruled out is primary reliance on electoral strategies or anything else that would encourage the illusion of a primarily electoral or parliamentary route to socialism.

Participation in electoral or parliamentary politics is

essentially a tactical and not a strategic question which, therefore, always admits of exceptions. But wherever possible or opted for, it has to be subordinated to extra-parliamentary class and mass politics, including the larger counter-hegemonic struggle against capitalism. People's power grows primarily out of such politics, out of their own activity, organisation and and struggle, as these come to be suffused with revolutionary consciousness. Following Lenin, Gramsci, is a good guide here. For him, participation in electoral or parliamentary politics is a tactical issue contingent on the strategic struggles centred on the class and mass organisations challenging the ruling class state. This relationship between strategic extra-parliamentary and tactical electoral politics must not be inverted. Nor the notion of revolutionary praxis is to be divorced from the self-organised and autonomous class struggle of the working masses in the name of 'flexible tactics', 'realism' and 'possibilism', or by raising the bogey of 'sectarianism', 'adventurism' or 'political immaturity'—formulas and phrases which social-democratic reformism has used over the years, all over the world, to rationalise class collaboration and justify or condone any and every kind of pragmatism, even opportunism on the terrain of bourgeois democratic politics.

It is necessary to recognise the decisive importance of extra-parliamentary class and mass politics for any renewed struggle for socialism, or for that matter, any sigificantly radical pro-people change in society. This is particularly necessary in view of the dismal failure of parliamentary politics in recent decades and globalisation's continued undermining of parliamentary-democratic institutions. It is not only that capital is powerful over society by virtue of its dominance in the economy, its power is further reinforced by the capitalist classes' ideology and personnel-wise domination of the various apparatuses of the state. This truly massive extra-parliamentary power of capitalism can only be matched by the working people's extra-parliamentary force and modes of action, their articulation in forms which are capable of offensive action against capitalism. It is significant that important economic or political 'gains' of the working people have almost invariably been the result of their reliance on 'extra-parliamentary' forms of struggle and organisation, whether in unions, protest movements, militant actions, or esewhere through the extra-electoral pressure they exercised on different institutions of the state. Indeed, to be at all effective, parliamentary politics itself has needed and today even more badly needs the radicalising pressure and support of extra-parliamentary politics. Beyond that, if the aim be socialism, it is unthinkable that the struggle for socialism can today at all advance without a radical reconstitution of the socialist movement as a strategically oriented and sustained extra-parliamentary mass movement capable of mounting an effective challenge to the capitalist powers that be.

Our emphasis on the importance of active extra parliamentary politics does not imply any kind of lawlessness, nor, as we have already clarified, an aprioristic rejection of electoral or parliamentary politics, But it does demand freeing of the working people's movement from the crippling constraints which the parliamentary 'rules of game' one-sidedly impose on it in the name of 'democratic polics'. It certainly rejects delusions of successful struggle against capitalism through parliamentary means. But it does not in any way pre-empt the issue of peaceful transition to socialism. Socialist politics, as we have insisted earlier, is not a matter of resorting to violence or picking up arms, which are purely tactical questions, though not to be dismissed on abstract moral grounds. Socialism is about a fundamental change in social production relations which a *real*, not merely juridical or formal social ownership of the means of production makes possible. And here, properly interpreted, Marx still remains the guide: 'peaceful if possible, with arms if necessary'. That is, it all depends on historical conditions and possibilities of the objective situation. A peaceful transition to socialism is of course the desirable thing. But the issue involved—peaceful or otherwise, or how peaceful—is really one for the ruling classes to respond to: are they willing to accept the people's peaceful, democratic verdict for socialism? As it is, these ruling classes have not even remotely shown this willingness so far. Instead they have invariably used their enormous economic and political power, often across countries, to thwart changes far, far less radical in nature than socialism. On has only to recall the overthrow of Mohammed Massadegh in Iran in 1953, of Arbenz in Guatemala in 1954, of Joao Goulart in Brazil in 1964, of Juan Bosch in the Dominican Republic in 1965, of Salvador Allande in Chile in 1973, and so on right up to the current efforts to overthrow Hugo Chavez in Venezuela or Evo Morales in Bolivia—all of them constitutional democratic regimes...

The world over any effort to seek radical or revolutionary change through democratic processes has been seen by the ruling classes as a challenge to capitalism or the established order and therefore too dangerous to be allowed to proceed. It has been regularly thwarted or destroyed. Defending America-backed armed intervention against democracy in Chile, Henry Kissinger declared: 'I don't see why we have to let a country go Marxist just because its people are irresponsible'. I will readily concede that democracy, bourgeois democracy to be precise, has often checked or corrected particular abuses of capitalism, made the struggle against its exploitation less painful, sometimes ratified victories that occurred elsewhere. But it has never yet led to the liberation of the oppressed classes.

Our experience with democracy in India has been no different. More than a decade back, in 1992, I had written:

> Obviously, democracy has not meant effective political power for the Indian people. Within almost two decades of Indian freedom and democracy, even so sympathetic a scholar as Gunnar Myrdal, a personal friend of Nehru, wrote of 'the new government's role

> as the successor to the British raj', of 'the gulf between rulers and ruled', and the life-style and conduct of the new rulers which 'encouraged the view that political independence had done little more than displace a foreign with a native privileged group', Pointing out that 'India is ruled by a select group of upper class citizens who use their political power to secure their privileged positions' and that 'the power struggle has mainly remained one between individuals and groups in the upper class in the broader sense', he concluded: 'Democracy has not enabled the majority of poor people to grasp, and organise themselves for utilising, political power to advance their own interests'. In 1973, V.K.R.V. Rao spoke of 'a political alliance of the intermediate classes with the upperclasses, resorting to socialist ideology only to win mass support but using all levers of power to facilitate a type of capitalist development in the interest of a narrow section of Indian society'; and fifteen years later he most emphatically stated that so far as 'the poor and deprived sections of the people' are concerned, 'parliamentary democracy has not been able to meet the challenge'.

The assessment still holds.

This however is not to reject the peaceful road to a socialist transformation which remains desirable. But if and when the people decide to travel the peaceful road, the principle is clear. This is how in his times, Cromwell, forced to make a revolution, put it: 'Trust in God, and keep your powder dry!' How people 'keep their powder dry' is not my concern at the moment. Only do it they must. What is involved is forging adequate extra-parliamentary sanctions to defend and enforce their democratic verdict, which includes preparedness to counter the inevitable 'slave-holders rebellion', as Marx had called it. Failure to do so will cost them dear, as it did the Chilean people in 1973. They failed to develop their own armed counterweight to defend their democratic verdict against the military coup which soon defied and overturned it and eventuated in a most brutal counter-revolution, massacre of virtually the entire Chilean Left including the democratically elected President Allende himself and the setting up of the notorious Pinochet dictatorship, all aided and abetted by the forces of international capital headed by the well-known defender and promoter of democracy in the world, the United States. I don't have to detail the lessons.

The issue of extra parliamentary sanctions involves recognition of the key question of revolutionary politics: the question of people's power in the state, their struggle for 'political supremacy' or state power which is central to revolutionary politics. There is no way a serious people's movement can avoid the question of political power. The real issue here is the concrete forms of struggle for it. This, obviously, cannot be settled beforehand; the objectives and the forms of struggle to be adopted, or combined, depend on the specific and ever changing historical circumstances. Even so, I would like to point out the essential inadequacy of 'civil society activism' (local or grassroots initiatives, social activism, NGOs, social movements, etc.), much lauded and advocated as a form of popular struggle these days. However admirable and welcome 'civil society activism' may be in many cases, the fact remains that, whatever be the subjective motivations of those involved, much local grassroots activity has come to be structured and appropriated by the ruling classes through the NGOs or other forms of 'social activism'. As intermediaries between the ruling elites above and the people below, NGOs and various forms of 'civil society initiatives' have served to effectively depoliticise the latter in the name of working for them. Imparting a pluralistic character to the on-going 'development', they have not only masked its monotonic reality as capitalist development but also helped rein in and depoliticise popular opposition to it. With their focus on management of life at ground level, major struggles over fundamental choices in economy or politics are, much in the manner of post-modernists, ruled out. The rhetoric over 'empowerment of people' conceals the fact that the state as the site of struggle stands abandoned and with it stands abandoned the struggle for political power which, obfuscations of bourgeois political theory notwithstanding, remains the preeminent form of power in society. 'Civil society activism' has generally served to delegitimise people-oriented politics and people's struggle for power in the state which revolutionary politics seeks and needs to seek.

To continue with the main argument: as suggested above, there are problems galore with participation in parliamentary politics. The critics have pointed their accusing finger at the Socialist and Communist Parties which, opting for parliamentary politics, have steadily slid into reformism. Such participation breeds 'parliamentary cretinism', a naive equation of electoral victory with winning of power, even with radical change itself, so that there is no need for or interest any longer in developing a militant revolutionary movement. Whatever movements exist or are built outside are subordinated to the 'struggle' inside the parliament. The electoral success is bought at the cost of an ideological backslide which has lasting deleterious effect. Operating on the terrain of bourgeois politics, responding to the issues it presents and accepting the choices it offers, entails a corruption of political consciousness and loss of revolutionary commitment and elan. Criticism of bourgeois parties for failing by their own standards – a staple of parliamentary politics– almost invariably leads to endorsing these standards yourself so that your original concerns come to be given a go-by. The process of making yourself electable on the terms set by the establishment leads to mirroring the establishment's view of the revolutionary Left who are now seen as an embarrassment, when not treated with plain hostility. Parliamentary politics, even as it corrupts in so many ways, exercises a most 'civilising' influence on revolutionaries, as Laski was fond of pointing out. It is no coincidence that the ruling classes looking for 'the most outstanding parliamentarians' or models of 'parliamentary rectitude' for their awards and honours have not unoften found them among leaders of Socialist or Communist Parties. They are hailed by the mainstream media as 'statesmen' for their role as the best custodians of bourgeois politics. And so on.

That the ruling classes have been eminently successful in using democracy, its rights and institutions agaist the people and for promoting their own class interests and that the greatest enemy of democratisation in the world today, the US, can hawk 'democracy' around the world in support of its imperialist politics makes parliamentary politics all the more suspect in the eyes of its critics.

The critics are fully justified in what they say, but their criticism does not add upto a justification for any kind of 'anti-parliamentary cretinism', the in-principle rejection of parliamentary politics by certain ultra-Left sections of the revolutionary movement.What we have here are problems that have to be confronted and resolved in terms of revolutionary vigilance in theory and practice and not evaded in a cretinous rejection of 'bourgeois democracy'. Parliamentary politics and electoral struggles are not to be rejected, or even treated as mere defensive tactics for the working people. They are today an integral part of any long revolution. They do not necessarily prevent a revolutionary movement or party from establishing and functioning on its own terrain, the terrain of independent class-based people's politics, which even as it confronts bourgeois politics on the latter's terrain, in parliament and outside, uses it to pose its own issues and choices, in its own way, before the people—not just for some electoral gains but real political advance. In other words, there is nothing in bourgeois democracy or parliamentary politics that in itself prevents its being subordinated to the extra-parliamentary politics of a revolutionary party or movement. Parties or movements are indeed coming up today, notably in Latin America, which are thus combining parliamentary and extra-parliamentary methods in pursuit of their revolutionary objectives.

The issue here is not commitment to democracy which has always been a vital part of the socialist agenda—and it is people who have fought for and won whatever democracy we have; and they need and value it most. Nor is it 'bourgeois democracy'. It is not even that parliamentary politics, as a form of politics, has its possibilities in the struggle for socialism and cannot be rejected so long as these possibilities remain unexhausted, not in your theory but in people's own practical experience, and, therefore, as a general principle, participation in parliamentary politics is necessary whenever and wherever possible–though exceptions to this principle are admissible in specific historical situations when people's interests, interests of their revolutionary movement so demand. The real issue here is an approach distant both from, ultra-Leftism on the one hand and from social democratic politics of accommodation on the other. It is the principle, but without any exception this time, that parliamentary politics needs always to be subordinated to extra-parliamentary class and mass politics. It can never be over-emphasised that people's power grows only out of such politics, out of their own activity, organisation and struggle as these come to be suffused with revolutionary socialist consciousness.

It may be added that participation in parliamentary politics does not by itself or necessarily means accepting the prevalent social order. Engels had categorically stated:

> the political freedom, the right of assembly and association and the freedom of the press–these are our weapons. Are we to sit back and abstain when somebody tries to rob us of them? It is said that a political act on our part implies that we accept the existing state of affairs. On the contrary, so long as this state of affairs offers us the means of protesting against it, our use of these means does not signify that we recognise the prevailing order.

These means, including participation in parliamentary politics, can in fact be used to redefine and extend the democratic parameters of the prevailing order in favour of the revolutionary movement, its extra-parliamentary struggles.

A Marxist perspective on the revolutionary process does not pose the issue of struggle for socialism, as its simplistic or ignorant critics think, in terms of violence or non-violence, or insurrectionist versus non-insurrectionist strategy. For it the real issue is an articulation and relationship between two terrains of struggle, that waged *within* the existing institutions of bourgeois democracy, and that waged *outside* them, in which the latter is always and ultimately the *decisive* terrain. Such was the perspective of Lenin, the principle underlying his notion of 'dual power'. Conceptualised by him in relation to the revolutionary process in Russia, 'dual power' has generally been taken to mean an adversary relation between a revolutionary movement operating in a revolutionary situation, and a bourgeois government under challenge from that movement. But it is suggestive of a more basic principle in relation to the two terrains of struggle mentioned above, in which the latter is always and ultimately the decisive terrain. This Leninist position still holds.

And here, while struggle within existing institutions remains a very important complement to the overall struggle, historical experience is, in its own way, quite instructive and needs to be taken note of. Details apart, what historical experience the world over points to is the paramount need to build up people's organised strength, a social power, on the terrain outside the established institutions of bourgeois democracy as necessary sanctions for the success of the revolutionary process. This will also be an important factor in determining how peaceful or 'non-violent' this revolutionary process is going to be.

Apropos our argument for participation in parliamentary politics and the desirability of peaceful socialist transformation, it is well to remember Marx's warning, hinted at earlier. Marx had warned that even in countries with the possibility of a relatively peaceful socialist revolution, the ruling classes will not give in without staging 'a slave holders revolt'. Urging the socialists to 'first win the great mass of the people',Engels had written:

> the time for surprise attacks, of revolutions carried out by small

> conscious minorities at the head of unconscious masses is past. When it is a question of complete transformation of the social organisation, the masses themselves must also be in it, must themselves already have grasped what is at stake, what they are going in for with body and soul.

Even so, he did not rule out a violent capitalist reaction to any peaceful bid for power— 'a blood-letting like that of 1871 in Paris'. The obvious implication is that extra-parliamentary struggles, the essential basis of any serious preparation to meet such a contingency, cannot and must not be subordinated to parliamentary politics. Mass extra-parliamentary socio-political movements and struggles indeed remain the central axis, the decisive terrain of the struggle for a socialist revolution. In fact capital is itself, by definition, and very effectively in its mode of acting and functioning, an extra-parliamentary force, and the capitalist state holds within itself any number of forces not amenable to the conventional democratic or parliamentary control. 'The "dominant class" is not a figure of speech', Miliband has pointed out, 'it denotes a very real and formidable concentration of power, a close partnership of capital and the capitalist state, a combined force of class power and state power, armed with vast resources, and determined to use them to the full, in conjuction with its allies abroad, to prevent an effective challenge to its power'. There will be no advance whatsover until the working people's movement is activated in the form of becoming capable of *offensive* action—as against the usual defensive action through conventional trade unionism, party politics in parliament or outside, etc.—against capital and the dominant classes through its own appropriate institutions and through its extra parliamentary force, its organised and conscious social power in society.

Here indeed also lies the answer to the question how violent or peaceful, armed insurrectionary or otherwise, the revolutionary process will be. Violence is not the essence of the matter and there is nothing un-Marxist or irrational in seeking to carry through a revolutionary process without violence or force of arms. But its possibility depends, above all, upon whether the ruling classes will allow it to be non-violent or peaceful. Historical experience, October Revolution included, bears witness that they will not. (Chile is a classic example in more recent times.) Even so, the greater the strength of the extra-parliamentary force or social power the revolutionaries have, the more evident their ability and willingness to meet counter-revolutionary violence with overwhelming revolutionary violence, the greater the chance that violence can be avoided and the revolutionary process be relatively peaceful.

The amount of violence that will be involved in a given revolutionary process is indeed impossible to predict in advance. It depends on the one hand on the nature and amount of ruling class resistance but in a large part, also, on how successfully the socialists have built people's social power from below and how hegemonic or influential they are in society as a whole. Socialists or communists, I may add, do not *advocate* violence. For them violence is a tragic necessity when the ruling classes violate the victories and rights of the people. People have a natural aversion to violence and revolutionaries respect it—a respect, as Trotsky has underlined in his account of the Russian Revolution, the Bolsheviks demonstrated remarkably in 1917.

•

We have travelled far and wide with our discussion of Indian politics and its path of development. One last word on the subject of 'development' to make a point which has been already made but is important enough to merit a separate, independent statement. We have argued that 'development' is not synonymous with capitalist development. We can well opt for a better, crisis-free and humane socialism-oriented development. But as something desirable, the concept of 'development' also raises what I have described as 'the overarching question as to what kinds of society we , as *human beings*, want to have'– a question in its own way implicit not only in Marx's critique of capitalism but also in the Webb's recognition of soviet achievement as 'a new civilisation', and the sickness of the 'over-developed' societies of advanced capitalism. Surely it is people and not 'economic growth' or 'productivity' that must come first in such a society. It has to be a humane society that fosters cooperation, solidarity and respect for universal ethical values, and makes for a non alienated, 'truly rich human life' that Marx spoke of. Of course such a society is impossible without basic material security and need satisfaction. But to believe that you can assure need satisfaction through greed, private acquistive drives, universal competition and strife and a production process which, as Marx said, turns worker into 'an automatic motor of a fractional operation' and 'cripples his body and mind'— the values and production process of capitalism— and yet hope for a humane society of cooperation and solidarity and social well-being, is utopianism of the worst kind. Subordinating humanity to economics, to imperatives of the market, capitalism commodifies life and undermines and rots away the relations between human beings which constitute societies. Its ethos of the market place – competition, egoism aggression, alienation, universal venality, in short the rat race—'its pseudo-moral principles', as Keynes once put it, 'which have hag-ridden us for 200 years (and) by which we have exalted some of the most distasteful of human qualities into the position of the highest virtues', create a moral vacuum in which nothing counts except what the individual wants and can grab, here and now. At the end of it all, even when wants are satisfied, the people are ever more subordinated, ever less free, ever more flattened and made passive by the dictatorship of consumerism that arbitrarily shapes values, imposing on them the heavy burden of uniformity. The values of difference, individualisation (not individualism), all-sided development of man, of human freedom itself, disappear in the market place which is proclaimed to be free. As *human beings*, people simply don't fit into capitalism. A capitalist society is not the society we want to have. However poor or backward today, we need to *move away* from capitalism-oriented development and, however slowly or falteringly, *move towards* building a humane, democratically functioning socialist society that fosters equality, cooperation, solidarity and respect for universal ethical values.

•

I had at the outset of my lecture spoken of the hard and fateful choices our people face today. One that encompasses them all (and which I have been discussing) concerns India's path of development. Do we accept the globalisation-dictated capitalist path of development our rulers have opted for, which polarises our people and further peripheralises them within a global capitalist system? Or do we struggle for a socialism-oriented development with its promise of a humane, democratic and ecologically respectful even if economically less prosperous society, providing a life of security and fulfilment for all?

It is my argument that we choose the latter. This implies, among other things, that we learn from the past experiences with economic development, avoid its negative consequences, for example, the damage that capitalist development regularly inflicts upon human beings and natural environment, that we reject the supposedly-Marxist fascination for the 'the development of production forces' that bedevilled the erstwhile 'socialist' economies and the obsession with 'economic growth' that plagues a capitalist economy, that we better negotiate the necessary trade-offs between economic development and social justice, between requirements of productivity or efficiency and environmental sustainability or quality of life which is not entirely a matter of material progress or economic growth. In other words, we have the opportunity 'to do something new', the all important option of a path of development which subordinating economy to humanity, plans and develops it in a way that is, in Marx's words, 'worthy of our human nature.'

Given the current balance of forces at the national level, it is likely that the struggle for this option will initially come up at the level of India's state politics. Apropos this perspective I would like to reproduce here a passage from what I wrote recently as a critical comment on the CPM politics in West Bengal:

> It is simply inconceivable that there can ever be a situation where socialist principles do not indicate what can be done and what should not be done in the light of these principles. With politics, that is people's politics, in command, socialism-oriented initiatives are indeed possible at the state and local levels in the Left-ruled states. The need is for the CPM to mobilise all the resources within and without the Left parties to work out an alternative path of development geared to the strategic goal of socialism, implement whatever part of it is implementable at the state and local levels in the states where the Left is in power, and mobilise the people elsewhere for it, with primacy given to extra-parliamentary struggles. This will make the Left-ruled states an example for the rest of the country and help the Party and the Left to rally all the radical forces in the country– NAPM, ultra-left formations, militant social movements and NGOs, etc. – to emerge as a genuine and effective alternative to the ruling class politics at the centre, with its own agenda of pro-people, self-reliant socialism-oriented development for the country. Of course, it is going to be long haul and we don't have to mix up our own mortality with a time-table for the achievement of socialist goals.

I know that this option, the struggle for a socialism-oriented development, means travelling along an uncharted road, and in a situation marked by an extraordinary dominance of capitalist ideology and an equally extraordinary inhibition of social imagination where our people, including those on the Left, seem to have lost the dreams they once had – the most terrible thing that can ever happen to a people – this option will be deemed impossible. But the situation demands nothing less, it indeed demands doing 'impossible' things. One recalls the adjuration of the students of Paris in their

May-June uprising of 1968. They had said: 'Be practical! Do the impossible!' Four decades later, it may be added: 'if we cannot do the impossible, we better prepare to face the unthinkable'. Some of the 'unthinkable' is already happening around us.

•

I would like to conclude with a brief comment addressed to the movement that Nagi Reddy was associated with, the revolutionary Left, born of India's communist movement and its heroic traditions — the Tebhaga agrarian movement, Telengana armed struggle, Naxallbari uprising, and so on — and now splintered into half a dozen odd parties and formations, each claiming to be the true communist party, 'the vanguard of the proletariat', and denouncing others as 'revisionists' of one kind or the other. The context of my argument here is the issue of alternaive revolutionary politics as I posed it sometime back in a critical comment on the CPM politics in West Bengal:

> An explicitly-stated strategic goal, distinct from and opposed to that of the ruling classes, and the struggle for this goal is what distinguishes revolutionary politics. It is this which gives effective meaning to the struggles of the working people, provides a purposeful direction to their political endeavours, and inspires them to 'attempt the impossible', 'to do something new'. Achieving this goal is invariably a long haul, but this has never deterred Communists from openly proclaiming and fighting for their goal..
>
> What is involved here is our vision of a just and humane society, beyond the present-day social orders, which I would still define as 'socialism', as the classical Marxist tradition viewed it. Holding on to this vision, 'Traum' Marx had called it, has been and remains integral to revolutionary politics.
>
> Towards the end of *What Is To Be Done*?—a text which is as relevant today as ever—Lenin, in the midst of the most hard-headed and unsentimental of polemics, quoted the journalist Pisarev:
>
> > if man were completely deprived of the ability to dream... if he could not from time to time run ahead and mentally conceive... the product to which his hands are only just beginning to lend

> shape, then I cannot at all imagine what stimulus there would be... (for) art, science, and political endeavour... The rift between reality and dreams causes no harm if only the person dreaming believes seriously in his dream, if he attentively observes life, compares his observations with his castles in the air... and works conscientiously for the achievement of his fantasies. If there is some connection between dreams and life then all is well.
>
> To which Lenin added:
>
> Of this kind of dreaming there is unfortunately too little in our movement. And the people most responsible for this are those who boast of their sober senses, their "closeness" to the "concrete".
>
> In the same text, Lenin had insisted: he, who forgets that 'the Communists support every revolutionary movement' and are for that reason obliged 'to expound and emphasise general democratic tasks before the whole people, *without for a moment concealing our socialistic convictions*', is not a Communist.
>
> What, then, is the Leninist 'dreaming' or vision of the CPM, the strategic goal of CPM politics; and how, and how openly or explicitly do they link their current political practices to this vision, the alternative strategic goal?

While one continues to hope that compulsions of the objective situation, pressure from below and the remnants of Marxism and socialist commitment within, may yet push or persuade the mainstream communist Left to recover its ability to dream and with it, its original promise to the Indian people, the future of this promise, it seems, is now linked to the future of the revolutionary Left. This Left can, if it wants, restore its lost honour to the word 'communist', once the proudest name in politics. It has the potential to offer our people the alternative revolutionary politics they need and are indeed looking for. But the realisation of this potential demands a fundamental reorientation of its politics and overcoming of its splintered state. It needs to abandon dogmas or orthodoxies of yester years (of both 'official Marxist' and 'Maoist' vintage) and return to Marxism of Karl Marx, to 'think as Marx would have thought in their place'—the only sense in which 'the word *Marxist* has any *raison d'etre'*, Engels had insisted. It needs to be *Marxist* in its assessment of what has happened in the Soviet Union and its implications. Still more, it has to assess its own past with the 'ruthless severity' and 'mercilessness', typical of Marx in matters of revolutionary theory and practice. There is the need for a concrete analysis of the changed and changing reality of India since 1947, and, given the growing regionalisation of Indian politics, also the need to work out, if I may put it this way, region or state specific versions of Lenin's *What Is To Be Done*? and *Where To Begin*? Above all, its splintered parties and formations need to unite on a platform of socialism-oriented politics with primacy for extra-parliamentary struggles. As they struggle to come together, at the very least, each party or formation needs to be genuinely self critical. They need to be fraternal towards each other and allow for differences over tactics, over forms or methods of struggle. Their polemics have to less jargonised and more principled, and not abusive or denunciatory ('revisionist' 'anarchist', etc.). They should talk *to* and not *at* each other, and for a change, also talk to the Indian people in a language the people understand. Even their criticism of the mainstream (communist) Left has to be less jargonised, better nuanced and persuasive —it has to be distinguishable from that of the Right (Congress, BJP. etc.) and in terms of an alternative revolutionary politics.

I know that this brief comment, asking for debate and struggle over so many sensitive issues, will not be welcome to many revolutionaries. But there is no denying the need for a theoretical renewal and a radical reorientation of the revolutionary Left's politics.

Unless the revolutionary Left thus comes together to offer a historically relevant alternative, a socialism-oriented alternative politics to the Indian people– and does so soon enough– its future in India is bleak. It will only further splinter and decline. It may continue to survive in its splintered areas of influence—this country has plenty of room for such ghettoised existence. But, as with the mainstream Left, it will cease to be any kind of Left force in Indian politics. 'History', Engels has said, 'is about the most cruel of all goddesses'. It has been cruel to Marx, Lenin and Mao and, in its own way, to Gandhi, Nehru and many others. It can be cruel to us, the revolutionary Left, too.

People will of course continue to fight. If they do not fight the right battles, they will fight the wrong ones—and this will be yet another tragedy for them and for the Communist Left in India.